THE CAMINO DE SANTIAGO SURVIVAL GUIDE

LOTUS EATERS TRAVEL

Copyright © 2023 LOTUS EATERS TRAVEL

All rights reserved

The characters and events portrayed in this book are fictitious. Any similarity to real persons, living or dead, is coincidental and not intended by the author.

No part of this book may be reproduced, or stored in a retrieval system, or transmitted in any form or by any means, electronic, mechanical, photocopying, recording, or otherwise, without express written permission of the publisher.

CONTENTS

Title Page

Copyright

Preface   5

Section One: Preparing For The Camino   8

Chapter One: Why walk the Camino de Santiago?   10

Chapter Two: What to Expect   29

Chapter Three: Picking your Camino route   43

Chapter Four: Training for the Camino   50

Chapter Five: Budgeting for the Camino de Santiago   62

Chapter Six: Packing for the Camino de Santiago   67

Chapter Seven: Frequently Asked Questions   81

Section Two: Walking The Camino   100

Chapter Eight: Albergue Guide   102

Chapter Nine: Socialising and Downtime   113

Chapter Ten: The Walking	119
Chapter Eleven: Staying Healthy On The Road	134
Chapter Twelve: Camino de Santiago daily stages	141
Chapter Thirteen: The Last 100km and the Camino Finisterre	155
Chapter Fourteen: What to do in Santiago de Compostela	180
Section Three: After The Camino	187
Chapter Fifteen: What next?	189
A message from Lotus Eaters Travel	209

Walking the Camino de Santiago: A Survival Guide

By Lotus Eaters Travel

Table of Contents

Prologue

Section One: Preparing for the Camino

- Chapter One: Why walk the Camino de Santiago?
- Chapter Two: What to expect
- Chapter Three: Picking a Camino route
- Chapter Four: Training for the Camino
- Chapter Five: Budgeting for the Camino
- Chapter Six: Packing for the Camino
- Chapter Seven: Frequently Asked Questions

Section Two: Walking the Camino

- Chapter Eight: Albergue guide
- Chapter Nine: Socialising and down time
- Chapter Ten: The walking
- Chapter Eleven: Staying healthy on the road
- Chapter Twelve: Route daily stages
- Chapter Thirteen: The last 100km and the Camino Finisterre

- Chapter Fourteen: What to do when you arrive in Santiago?

Section Three: After the Camino

- Chapter Fifteen: What next?

PREFACE

Until 2021, I had not heard of the Camino de Santiago. I was having drinks with some new friends, when they started talking about the "Camino", which they had walked together as a couple in 2019 before the global Covid Pandemic hit. Colloquially referred to as the "Camino", they spoke of "Albergues", meeting other walkers (many of whom sounded like absolute characters), epic scenery and what seemed to be a totally amazing adventure. But, I had (mostly) no idea what they were talking about, it was like a whole new language. One of these "if you know, you know" situations.

Then in early 2022, I had made a decision to take some time out of my job in the busy corporate world in London. After the pandemic, ten plus years of working for other people, and some personal events, I needed some space to ventilate. My partner and I (Pinky and Brain style) decided that we needed to take over the world together, one amazing travel experience at a time. I distinctly remember the moment that we realised the Camino had to be our first stop. We were in

Costa Rica and had just hiked 15km in the midday sun, with our luggage on our backs. We arrived to a bar, sunk down a refreshing beer each and it hit us, we needed to do the Camino. We were craving freedom, adventure, exercise and nature. The Camino had to be the answer.

The next six months went by in a whirlwind. We packed up our houses, sorted out our personal affects and I informed my employer about my decision. It was such a haze, with so much to do, that we really didn't get any time to plan our Camino experience. We just got on a plane with our rucksacks, and we were on our way. There are pros and cons to this approach, but looking back, I really wish that there had been a one stop guide to help us prepare and walk the Camino. Hence, three Camino's later, I am now writing this Survival Guide in the hope that it helps you to get the most from your Camino experience!

SECTION ONE: PREPARING FOR THE CAMINO

"I will prepare and someday my chance will come." — Abraham Lincoln.

CHAPTER ONE: WHY WALK THE CAMINO DE SANTIAGO?

As I write this, I am sitting in the shadow of the Camino de Santiago Cathedral and watching each Pilgrim walking into this auspicious place. I am filled with awe as I notice the look on all their faces. A mix of joy, satisfaction, pure unadulterated relief and of course, pain. Some reach the Cathedral alone, by their own choice. Others are in groups of old friends, or new friends alike. Couples stand posing for pictures or gazing into each other's eyes with astonishment. Every single person has been on a journey and as they arrive at the Cathedral in Santiago, it becomes completely clear that they are now part of a uniquely special and captivating community.

This is why you must walk the Camino once in your life. I will go into that in more detail later in this book, but first, let's start with a little background to the Camino de Santiago.

The Camino de Santiago, quite literally means "The way of Saint James." In 820, a tomb was discovered in Galicia that was thought to contain the remains of St James the Great (Santiago in Spanish). The details surrounding this are slightly hazy, but it is widely accepted that this marks the beginning of Christians making a Pilgrimage to the tomb of St James. According to research conducted by the Museum of Pilgrims in Santiago, it was "the act of this pilgrimage that led to the birth of the Camino". It is believed that the Frenchman, Bretanaldo, who walked the Camino in 920 is the first known foreign Pilgrim to have taken the journey to Santiago.[i]

As they say, the rest is history! And today, the Camino is thriving. In 2022, 438,683[ii] people completed the Camino taking various routes and by several different means. In 2023 already (April 2023 at time of writing), 38,000 people have crossed the finish line in Santiago. The vast majority walk (94.5% in 2022)[iii], but the Camino can be completed on bicycle, horseback, sailboat and in a wheelchair if required. This book focuses mainly on how to walk the Camino, because that is our area of expertise, but much of the guidance could be used to help cyclists on their way.

Glossary

First, let's get clued up on the lingo!

Camino: Literally "The Way", used colloquially instead of Camino de Santiago. But be aware there are other Camino's in different countries!

The Way: As above, literal translation of "Camino." Often used by Pilgrims to indicate the journey that they are on, physically, spirituality and emotionally. For example, "I am on my way."

Pilgrim: A Pilgrim is someone making the pilgrimage to Santiago on the Camino. You will also hear "Peregrinos", which means Pilgrims in Spanish.

Albergue: An Albergue is a hostel, normally these are for exclusive use of Pilgrims walking the Camino.

Yellow Arrows: All along the Camino routes, you will see yellow arrows de-marking "the way". These arrows are widely thought to have been painted in the 1980s and are maintained by various associations that are friends of the Camino.

The Shell: A scallop shell that many Pilgrims choose to fix to their bags to demonstrate that they are walking the Camino (just in case the raggy clothes and dishevelled hair isn't enough to give it away!)

Credential: The Credential or "credencial", is an accreditation document given to Pilgrims at the start of their journey. It is available digitally or as a physical certificate and you need it to gain access to Albergues. As you travel along the Camino, you will collect stamps which show how far you've travelled. This makes a pretty cool souvenir! You can collect your credential at most Camino start points, ask in Albergues or Cathedrals.

Compostela: The Compostela was the original accreditation provided to Pilgrims who had journeyed to visit the tomb of St James. Today, you can obtain the Compostela (a certificate) when you reach Santiago, if you can prove that you walked the last 100km or cycled the last 200km (by obtaining a minimum of two stamps per day in your credential card) and if you travel the Camino for religious reasons.

Certificate of Distance: This is a certificate you can obtain at the Pilgrim's reception office in Santiago which shows how far you have walked and in what time period. You will need to pay a few euros if you want to collect a certificate.

The Routes

Next, I'll give you a quick overview of the routes (we will go into more detail on this in later chapters,) but a brief overview will help to set the next few chapters in context.

The French (Frances) Way

This route is the most commonly taken today, it starts in Roncesvalles and passes through Pamplona, Logrono, Burgos and eventually enters Galicia. The total distance is 780km.

The Northern (Norte) Way

It starts in Irun and meanders through San Sebastián, Bilbao, Santander, Gijón and enters Galicia at Ribadeo. The total distance is 835km.

The Primitive (Primitivo) Way

This route commences in Oviedo and heads to Santiago inland through Asturias, before joining the French/Northern ways towards the end. The total distance is 321km.

The English (Ingles) Way

This route starts in either Coruna or Ferrol and ends in Santiago. It is named after the Pilgrims who originally travelled from the United Kingdom. The distance from Ferrol is 110km and 75km from Coruna.

The Portuguese Way

This route s starts in either Lisbon or Porto (Porto most commonly) and enters Spain in Tui. There is a Portuguese inland route or a coastal route, which is slightly longer. From Lisbon, the inland route is 600km and the coastal 620km. From Porto, the inland route is 230km and the coastal route is 260km.

The Vía de la Plata

This route starts in Seville and passes inland before joining Galicia. The distance is a cool 1000km.

Why should you walk the Camino de Santiago?

At its original inception, the Camino was a literal "pilgrimage". Those who walked it, did so for religious purposes. Today, some do still walk the way for that very same reason. In my experience, this isn't often spoken about, with those who are following a religious path perhaps choosing to maintain a sense of privacy. According to the official statistics, in 2021 36% of Pilgrims completed the Camino for religious reasons and 43 % for religious and "other"[iv]. This data is based on self-declaration, so it is difficult to prove the true accuracy of the numbers. This leaves around 20% of Pilgrims declaring that they completed the Camino for non-religious purposes.

One of the reasons that many people choose to walk a thru-hike like the Camino, is to seek transformation in their lives. Certainly, for me this was one of the main reasons that I decided to walk my first Camino. It's also one of the reasons that I continue to walk long-distance hikes today.

Why thru hiking is the ultimate transformation travel?

> **"Meet me there, where the sea meets the sky, Lost but finally free."**

Raynor Winn, The Salt Path

The Salt Path by is one of the most thought-provoking books that I've ever read. The reason that The Salt Path was so thought provoking for me, was that it is a story about thru-hiking and the transformative power that long distance walking has. For anyone who hasn't heard of The Salt Path, it is the story of Raynor and her husband, referred to affectionately as "Moth" throughout. The couple find themselves homeless, at an unlikely time in their lives in their 50s and make the brave decision to walk the Southwest Coastal Path in England.

I say "brave decision," but it is clear from reading the book that they felt as though they had little option. With no money, no home, and no employment (their livelihood was their former home) the pull of the path called to them. Perhaps because the only other "option" was to live on the streets. But through their epic walk around the Southwest Coast of England they found something that they didn't expect. They found a place to be each day. They found somewhere they belonged, a routine and a challenge that fulfilled them.

"Lying in the sun on baking-hot grass, having walked four miles before lunch and eaten a handful of elderberries straight from the tree, there's a lot to be said for being a vagrant."

Raynor Winn, The Salt Path

It really is a great read, a page turner, not least because I wanted to find out whether Raynor and Moth made it to the end of their 630-mile trek. But what I was particularly struck by as I finished this book, was the feeling that I got. We all know the feeling when you finish a great book. There's a sense of achievement, you've learnt something new, you've met some new characters, but overall, you're quite sad that it's over. This reminded me of the exact bundle of feelings that I got whe I finished my first Camino de Santiago.

How does thru-hiking change you?

> **"In every walk with nature, one receives far more than he seeks"**
>
> John Muir

A better question might be, how doesn't thru-hiking change you? Really, thru-hiking will change and transform you as much as you let it.

You can, of course, choose to just enjoy the experience of thru-hiking. Perhaps you become fitter physically, and that's it. Perhaps walking the Camino de Santiago becomes a distant but fond and valued memory. Or simply an anecdote that you can reel off at the pub in 30 years' time. But you might also find the transformative power of thru-hiking, if you want to and if you let it in.

Many people talk of finishing a thru-hike, such

as the Camino or the Pacific Coast Trail in the USA and realising that they aren't at the end. Yes, they've finished the walk that they set out to do. But instead of feeling that they've completed a mission, they've discovered something new. They've found a door and they've opened it and now it's open they can't shut it again. Like a gleeful can of worms. At this point, perhaps the transformation they find is that they want to keep walking and they sign up to do another thru hike immediately. There's a reason that "thru-hiking" and the Camino de Santiago has a bit of a cult status.

Others may find something else that they've been looking for when tackling a thru-hike. Maybe they meet their one great love, or somebody that transforms their life or takes it into a new direction. Perhaps, like Cheryl Strayed in Wild, they find the answers to questions they've been looking for. Taking the time to soul-search and redirect their lives, change tracks if you will.

Capability and resilience

It is quite difficult to start a long-distance thru-hike, like the Camino and finish it as the same identical person that you were at the start. A thru-hike is a challenge and completing it might teach us lessons about ourselves, about how our capacity, our capability or our resilience is greater than we thought or anticipated.

> **"I was amazed that what I needed to survive could be carried on my back. And, most surprising of all, that I could carry it."**

Cheryl Strayed, Wild

I love this quote from Wild, because it speaks to two huge transformations that we undergo on a thru-hike like the Camino. We realise that we don't need anything but what we can fit in our backpacks. Walking a long-distance trek starts a new journey towards minimalism for many, or indeed consolidates minimalist leanings that they may have harboured all their lives. But, as Cheryl says here, we also realise that we our bodies are more capable than we think. We have all the strength that we need within.

Thru-hiking and body transformation

There's a lovely part of The Salt Path when Raynor comes out of the shower and thinks that she's being confronted by a stranger in the campsite toilet block. The stranger is in fact her own reflection in the mirror, but she doesn't recognise the person that she has become in such as short space of time.

> **"A woman on the other side of the room looked up at me: hair like a bird's nest, burnt brown face with a shredded red nose, red calloused feet, lean athletic legs and ribs poking through saggy flesh."**

Raynor Winn, The Salt Path

When I googled thru-hiking as part of the research for this book, I found oodles of results for "thru-hiking before and after," and then thousands of pictures of men and women before and after thru-hikes. Without fail, all of them look slimmer, more lean and more toned. Thru-hiking can have huge transformational impacts on your body and your physical being.

Not all of these are good. Personally, a bit like Raynor, I ended up with a bird's nest on my head after walking my first Camino. My hair is still in the recovery position. However, in general, the transformation that your body can undergo during a thru-hike is significant and positive. Muscles will become stronger, cardiovascular systems will improve and weight will be lost.

Physical recovery

In fact, in the Salt Path, Moth who had been diagnosed with a degenerative disease, finds that his health improves during the thru-hike, despite medical professionals refusing to accept this. Moth refers to the walk as an "extreme form of physio" and quips that "maybe I'll have to keep walking all of my life."

I'm with Moth on this. Of course not nearly as serious as Moth's illness, but during my first Camino de Santiago thru-hike I overcame a gnarly knee injury that I had spent years in physio trying to resolve. My partner and I both felt fitter than ever when we arrived in Santiago. Fit and full of life. This can be an addictive result of thru-hiking, because when (or if) we go back to our normal daily lives, sitting at a computer or on the sofa for hours on end, we might find the fleshy dough creeping back onto our bodies like a familiar, but unwelcome friend.

Everything is impermanent.

"Me thinks that the moment my legs begin to move, my thoughts begin to flow."

Henry David Thoreau

One of my favourite things about thru-hiking and the Camino de Santiago particularly, is the predictability of it. That may sound dull. Isn't thru-hiking supposed to be a thrill seekers adventure? Who wants predictable?

But predictable can be good. No fuss and no muss. When the sun rises you head out, boots hit the ground, backpack hoists up and off you go. Then there's a joyful lunch break, a few cups of coffee and a few more miles. At the end of the day, the sun sets on somebody who feels satisfied, sweetly tired and sated.

But what is so wonderfully enriching and, here's that word again, transformative, about this predictable thru-hiking routine is that it reminds you that everything is impermanent. As you march on along the path, as the miles add up, as the sun rises and sets, everything is changing. Time is passing.

Every person you meet, every scenic vista, every satisfying sip of water, every painful step –it is all temporary. And that's OK. Because as soon as you realise this, you can enjoy it.

Who should try thru-hiking on the Camino?

"Were we searching this narrow margin between the land and the sea for another way of being, becoming edgelanders along the way. Stuck between one world and the next. Walking a thin line between tame and wild, lost and found, life and death. At the edge of existence."

Raynor Winn, The Salt Path

Thru-hiking, and the Camino, really can be for anybody. It is not an exclusive club for the super-fit, or indeed the super-wealthy. You can do it on a budget, or on a total shoestring (as Raynor and Moth did). You can also train to prepare for it, or you can just gradually build up to the bigger routes.

One of my favourite blogs, Camino Stories *(www.storiesfromthecamino.com)* is filled with tales of normal people who have taken on the Camino. Anyone even considering doing it should peruse this and read just a few stories of thru-hiking transformation. I challenge you to not feel just a little bit inspired.

Whether you're an empty nester like Carolyn Gillespie, author of Pilgrim Finding a New Way on the Camino de Santiago, undergoing significant life changes like Raynor and Moth, searching for something like Cheryl or grieving like Michael Sheen in The Way–thru-hikes are there for you. So why not give it a go in 2023?

Ten reasons why you should walk the Camino de Santiago

If that's not enough for you, here are ten reasons why you should walk the Camino de Santiago.

For the purpose of this book, I am not going to refer to religion as a reason to walk the Camino. If that is your motivation, then I expect that you will have already considered this.

One: A break from reality

Walking the Camino means you will not have time to scroll through Instagram or interact with the 24/7 news headlines. It's a readymade digital detox. Your daily routine on the Camino also means you quickly fall out of the "norm", and if you want to take a complete exit from your previous reality, then this is your opportunity. Forget disappearing to an Ashram in India, the Camino has you covered for total escapism.

Two: Emotional and mental challenge

You'll have a lot of thinking time, which means you have time to explore all of those deep-seated emotions or to contemplate any existential questions that may be lingering in your mind. I met people on the Camino who cried for the first time in a long time. And others who felt they needed the time to process after a breakup or to consider a new career change. Whatever you are contemplating, the combination of walking and isolation, is bound to bring up challenges for everyone.

Three: Physical challenge

Many Camino "purists" will say that you've missed the meaning of the Camino if you just do it for the physical challenge. I disagree. The physical gruel of the longer routes is not to be taken lightly and if you want to complete it, you'll need to dig deep. Whether you're cracking out 40 km a day, or taking it slower, your body is bound to have undergone some sort of transformation by the time you reach Santiago.

Four: The people you meet

After being locked away during the Pandemic, this was one of my key reasons for walking the Camino. Every day, you get to meet totally new people if you choose to. You can also find lifelong friends, tagging on to a "Camino family" and sharing the whole journey together. You may start walking as strangers, but after a few hours of hiking together, you are bound to become friends.

Five: The Camino is a community

"Pilgrims", or those walking the Camino are a protected group in Spain. The locals are (mostly) very friendly and supportive of pilgrims, with strangers regularly wishing you "Buen Camino" as you walk by. Fellow pilgrims are also super friendly and diverse. You'll meet people of all nationalities and backgrounds, and everyone is embraced. Once you're in the Camino club, you're in it for life!

Six: Scenery and exploring

Exploring by foot means you will get to see Spain through a different lens. On the North Route, you'll find beaches that are only accessible by footpath. You'll also walk through remote towns and villages that otherwise would not be found on the tourist trail and they all have something unique to offer. Not to mention, the fantastic mountain scenery. Watching the sun rise, after you've hiked up a massive hill at dawn is something you will never forget.

Seven: Freedom

On the Camino, it's just you and your backpack. Unless you opt to use the bag carrying service (which may suit some people), you will be responsible for carting your belongings about as you walk. I would strongly advise that you pack light! Not only will this save you from crippling back pain but will give you a sense of freedom that is difficult to achieve otherwise. If you want to know what it's like to live with only a few belongings and zero home comforts, then the Camino can help you.

Eight: Value for money

Walking the Camino can be excellent value for money. Municipal Albergue's will cost you around 10 euros per night, and there are some "Donativo" (donate what you can) options too. Some Albergue's will provide a cheap communal meal, others have kitchens so you can cook a basic dinner. Supermarkets are readily available, so you can easily prepare packed lunches too. A glass of wine or beer will set you back only around 2 euros too! Comparative to other "adventure tourism" options, where you might be paying for a guide of for someone to organise things for you, the Camino is excellent value for money.

Nine: Romance

If you're single when you walk the Camino, there are lots of opportunities to meet likeminded adventurers. There are new romantic connections being formed every day out on the trails. We met so many new couples, or people enjoying a short fling. If you take on the Camino as a couple, it's bound to strengthen your relationship. Walking all day may not sound romantic, but the shared experience and quiet unique moments you enjoy together are truly special.

Ten: It's fun

You'll laugh, you may cry. You'll be hungry, sweaty, and pretty dirty. Your feet will probably be covered in blisters and some nights you won't sleep at all. But you will have terrific fun along the way!

CHAPTER TWO: WHAT TO EXPECT

In this chapter, I will provide a bit more information to help set your expectations about walking the Camino de Santiago. We will cover, what to expect, the types of people you're likely to meet and some key facts to help you impress the friends that you will inevitably make along the way.

What you need to know before you walk the Camino

It is a physical challenge

If you choose to walk the Primitivo, the Norte, the Frances or the Portuguese you are likely to experience some level of physical challenge. Walking 20km on a weekend might feel like an easy thing to do, but walking 20km or more every day over one month, will challenge you. I am yet to meet anyone who has not experienced an aspect of physical hardship whilst walking the Camino. Whether it be foot pain, knee pain, new injuries, shoulder pain, pulled hamstring, you name it, it will happen at some point. You can prepare for it and try to mitigate this risk (more in later chapters).

It will challenge you in other ways too

Aside from the risk of physical injury, some days will just be hard. You might have had a bad night's sleep, the weather could be awful or the sun may be extremely hot. You may get tonsillitis, or a sudden vomiting bug, even Covid. Perhaps the social side will challenge you and you'll need some alone time. Or, you get fed up of smelling gross and wearing the same clothes. Things will come up. But you'll get through them and keep going and be laughing in no time!

You'll probably get blisters

This is pretty much an inevitability. Fool proof blister socks or not. You'll get one or two. Pack blister plasters, but be prepared that you may have days when its painful to walk. I'd also recommend reading up on blister management so you can ensure they don't get infected and you know how to treat different kinds of blisters. I'm no expert, but it cannot hurt to come armed with a needle (sterilised of course) to pop any blisters that are preventing you from walking. Unless you are willing to quit at the first sign of a blister, you'll need a solution to manage any that appear.

It will probably rain

You will be walking in Spain or Portugal – should you really expect rain? Yes! Summer on the Northern Route almost guarantees some rain. Santiago is in the Northern part of Spain, the weather in Finsiterra can be notoriously iffy. It will rain, sometimes hard. If you're lucky it'll be in the evening when you're at your Albergue. If you're less lucky it'll be when you're on the top of a hill which will turn into a mud path very quickly.

You'll be able to carry less than you think

Something I discovered quickly! Yes, you want to pack all your essentials, but a heavy bag will slow you down and cause injury. Err on the side of caution. What you can carry for 10 minutes, is not the same as what you can carry for 30 days straight. In a later chapter, we will cover more on packing advice. But, it's important to be aware before you go that you are going to have to live without most home comforts for the period of time in which you are walking the Camino. You will have limited clothing and you are just going to have to get used to that. Look at it as an opportunity to try out that whole French Capsule Wardrobe thing.

People will snore

Most people walking the Camino (the independent way) will stay in Albergues in a dormitory sleeping arrangement. Be prepared that every dorm will have at least one snorer. Often, you will be serenaded to sleep by a veritable chorus of snoring, it will not be musical! If you are somebody who needs a lot of sleep, a light sleeper or just down right impatient, then you will find this difficult. There are ways to mitigate the impact (ear plugs, headphones, or private rooms if you are able to afford this.)

Bed bugs are real

I'm not trying to gross you out, but you should be aware that bed bugs can be an issue on the Camino. According to my research, the later you are in season, the more likely that bed bugs will be an issue. If you think about it, Albergues have a high turn over (normally a new person in each bed every night). Often, the buildings are not that clean and often the people sleeping in the beds aren't either. Bed bugs are a logical consequence. If you get bed bugs, you'll need to act quickly (wash all of your belongings). But you can prevent it, as far as possible, by taking your own sleeping bag or sheet and of course, keeping up good hygiene practises.

Sometimes you will need to book accommodation

This is a bit of a bummer as I think it's removed a bit of the spontaneity of walking the Camino. It's not always the case, but there are bottle necks on the way that mean everyone has to stay in one town. A couple of Albergues have shut their doors since Covid, so the choices are more limited. Call ahead the day before, or on the day, or check booking.com. Or if you can't book and you know it's going to be a busy Albergue, make sure you get there early. This is particularly an issue on the Norte, as there are less Albergues, and sometimes on the Portuguese. I'm not sure why, but on the Portuguese route, I noticed that most people booked ahead for every day. The Frances route has an abundance of accommodation, although it is the busiest route, accommodation booking is less of an issue.

Everyone is so friendly

Perhaps it's because there is a shared sense of mission, or that Pilgrims are quite like minded. But everyone you meet, pretty much without exception will be super friendly. People will want to get to know you and walk with you. It won't be considered unusual to just start talking to strangers. And it's not strange to get to know people on the Camino really quickly. Many people end up having more intimate conversations with people they've known for a matter of days whilst walking the Camino, than they ever might with their own family.

You'll never walk alone

You can walk alone if you want, but you don't have

to. I would say that there are very few stretches of the Camino where you won't see people regularly (unless you walk in Winter). This means that it feels fairly safe for solo travellers. If you want to join a group and walk all day, or just walk and talk for a few kms, then that's OK too. Even if you join the Camino as a solo walker, you will not end up solo, unless you make the decision to do so.

You'll have a lot of thinking time

Even if you choose to walk the Camino with others (whether new friends or old), you will still have a lot of time to think. If you walk around 25km per day, that's five to six hours of just putting one foot in front of the other. You'll also have time in the evening in the Albergue, as well as time when you are laying in your bunk listening to the sweet sound of snoring! This means, that walking the Camino, can be a really good time to work through some things in your mind. Whether you have big existential questions to address, or small decisions to make, you'll have the time to consider it all. I'll talk more about how I used a journaling practise to make the most of my experience in a later chapter.

Who can you expect to meet on the Camino?

This was a big question I had prior to walking my first Camino. I had absolutely no idea what to expect. The answer is you really can meet just about anyone. This is a fascinating thing about walking the Camino, it attracts people from all walks of life. I met people from around the world, Israel, Italy, Austria, Germany, Australia, Spain, Ukraine, USA, even Brazil. According to the official statistics from 2022, the vast majority of those completing the Camino are Spanish, a massive 54%, followed by Italian 6%, American (USA) 6%, German 5% and Portuguese 4%[v]. In 2021, and in previous years, the gender split was roughly 50% male and 50% women[vi]. In terms of ages, the Camino also welcomes all! I've met so many people in their late 60s, and some who were under 20. The statistics show that in 2021, 26% of those on the Camino were under 30, with 16% over 60 and the remainder between 30 and 60[vii].

You'll get the most out of the Camino experience if you talk to many people, regardless of background or language. Google Translate, can be helpful to break down language barriers.

Seven Types of People You'll Meet On The Camino

To help you get a sense of who you might meet, here's a slightly satirical look at the different Camino archetypes.

One: The Young Guns

The young guns are on a gap year, or on summer holidays from university. They are footloose and fancy free. They can be found chatting late into the night, socialising and maybe enjoying a few drinks. But this doesn't stop them in the morning! They'll be first out the blocks at 0600. Or if they're not, they will soon be catching up with you as they walk as fast as their young legs can carry them. They remain miraculously injury free, bar a few pesky blisters. They sleep soundly, never waking up in the night for a pee! And, they are, oh so, optimistic! You can't help but have a smile on your face when you meet one.

Two: The Old Timers

The Old Timers are out on the Camino representing their generation. They are the O.Gs. Many are in their 60s or 70s and they are owning it. But the old timers are not to be underestimated – they are speedy. Just when you think you've overtaken one, you stop for a 5 minute break and they are hot on your heels. They walk with an air or wisdom and authority and are full of useful bits of advice for other walkers. Long may the old timers keep on walking!

Three: The Casanovas

A subset of the Young Guns (for the most part). This group are ostensibly walking the Camino. But really, they are hunting for some transient romance. Find them chatting to the nearest singletons, revelling in their favourite flirtatious stories night after night.

Four: The Camino Die Hards

This is not their first rodeo. The Camino Die Hards have been here before. They've walked the Primitivo, they've walked the Frances, hell they've probably walked all the routes backwards with a blindfold. They are the Camino Oracles. A few have Camino tattoos, some have matted hair and bongs, others have settled for sewing various Camino badges to their hiking bags. Make sure you chat to the Camino Die Hards. They've got some wonderful stories to tell.

Five: The Logisticians

Oh the Logisticians! These people are the recovering "Type A" personalities. They've probably chosen to walk the Camino to get away from work and their non-stop busy lives. But, find themselves on the Camino using all the apps and maps to plan each day carefully. They'll be combing the Google reviews, aiming only for top-rated accommodation and restaurants. They will even seek out other Logisticians to compare notes. We would all be lost without them!

Six: The Couples

The Couples are doing their own thing. They'll dip in and out of the Albergues, sometimes opting for private rooms for "couple time". They will socialise, but sometimes they will indulge in a romantic (private) dinner. You may also find them having massive arguments on the roadside.

Always good entertainment!

Seven: The Plastic Fantastics

Find them on the last 100km of the Camino. They tend to carry big bags, even though they're only joining for a short stretch. Groups of them, hoards in fact, will descend. Often they will blast loud music from their backpacks and stop to take all the selfies. They've got blisters upon blisters from their brand new hiking boots. But hey, they're bringing the party vibes and much needed blast of new energy. Plus, they smell way better than the rest of us!

10 Facts About the Camino To Impress Your Friends

Whoever you meet, you're sure to impress them with these 10 facts about the Camino:

One: Where is the 0km Marker

Once you enter Galicia, you'll notice that the way markers count down the number of kms to Santiago. But, you will not find a 0km way marker stone in Santiago. In fact, the only 0km marker stone is on the Cape of Finisterra.

Two: The origin of the arrows

The yellow arrows first appeared in 1980, and it is believed that they were painted by a Priest. Since this date, they have been maintained by various associations that regard themselves as friends of the Camino. Without them, we would all be lost!

Three: Legend of the Vakner

When walking the Camino to Finisterre, you can see a statue of the "Vakner". This a mythological creature first spotted in 1491 by Pilgrims walking to Finisterre. It is claimed that these ferocious creatures would prevent the journey to Finisterre.

Four: Famous Pilgrims

Many famous people have completed parts of the Camino de Santiago, including Jenna Bush (the daughter of George W Bush), the King and Queen of Belgium and Martin Sheen.[viii]

Five: A backpack once travelled the Camino

In 2020, to keep the Camino alive during the Pandemic, a backpack travelled the French route (supported by two humans!) This was called "Light of the way" and there is a book written about it.

Six: Movies about the Camino

The most famous is "The Way", which debuted in 2011 and starred Martin Sheen.

Seven: The quickest anyone has ever completed the French route

The fastest known time for completing the French route of the Camino is reported to be approx 6 days (male record) and 9 days (female record), these times are contested in ultra-running circles, but are generally the only known "fastest times.[ix]

Eight: Why the last 100km is significant

The two most popular start points for the Camino de Santiago are both 100km away from the city, if you don't walk the entire 100km into Santiago (or cycle the last 200km), then you will not be awarded the Compostela. This gives the last 100km significance, but also means that it gets jolly busy!

Nine: The history of Finisterre

In Roman times, it was believed that Finisterre was the edge of the world. Finisterre in Latin (Finis Terrea), literally means the end of the world. Since then, Pilgrims have descended to Finisterre, believing that it is the "metaphorical" end. For years, many Pilgrims would burn personal items once they reached Finisterre – this may have been a ritual to mark the end of the road or alternatively (and a bit grimly) this was to burn all the bed bugs in their clothing.

Ten: The meaning of the shell

The scallop shell, was historically sold in Santiago Cathedral and was seen as as symbolically similar to a hand and therefore representative of God's deeds.[x] Other's claim that the shell represents Galician culture, with strong links to the seafood industry. Nowadays, you can buy them along the route and tie them to your bag!

CHAPTER THREE: PICKING YOUR CAMINO ROUTE

Which route to take

Probably one of the first decisions you have to make when preparing for the Camino is deciding which route to take. Here's a guide to help you to narrow down this decision:

How long do you have?

The first key question is how much time you have. Perhaps you're a teacher with the entire summer holidays stretching out in front of you, or you've just got one week of annual leave.

One Week or Less: If you've only got one week or less on this occasion, then I'd say you have a few options. Either, walk the last 100km into Santiago along the Camino Frances. This means you get to experience the atmosphere, you get to enter Santiago and you can officially collect a certificate for walking the last 100km! If you're a fast walker and you have a full week, you may be able to get to Finisterre (the end of the world!) on the West Coast of Spain. If you're looking for something different, then you could walk a stretch of the Camino del Norte – San Sebastian to Bilbao is popular and would be a great way to see two fab cities!

There's a whole chapter later in this book dedicated to the last 100kms of the Camino de Santiago, so you can read an in-depth description of each

Two Weeks: With a full two week stint, I'd recommend the Camino Portuguese. You can walk the 230km from Porto to Santiago comfortably within 14 days. If you're looking for a more challenging terrain, then try the Camino Primitivo – with a bit of speed behind you, then you should cover it in two weeks.

One Month: With one month or more to play with, you can choose any route you like! The Camino del Norte or Camino Frances are most popular with those who have 30 days to cover them. But, completely dependent on how far you want to walk each day (see below!)

How far do you want to walk each day?

Next, consider how far you can realistically walk each day. We will cover training in a bit more detail, but before you decide on route, it's worth having a realistic idea (based on trials) of how far you think you can cover each day.

10 to 15km: If you want to keep the kms per day down under 15km, then you will need to either i) Pick a shorter route (such as the Portuguese route from Porto) or ii) ensure you have enough time. If you want to take the Camino del Norte for example, you'll need to allow at least 8 weeks at this pace.

15 to 25km: If you're aiming to walk between 15 and 25km per day, then you should be able to cover one of the long routes in about 6 weeks. Or, opt for a shorter route if you have less time than that.

25km+ : If you're willing to walk in excess of 25km per day, then all routes are open to you. On the Camino del Norte, I had some days where I had to walk 40km to find accommodation, but other days where 25km was more the norm!

What kind of ambience are you looking for?

Quiet Isolation: If you want total peace and isolation, then you have a couple of choices. Either, pick one of the main routes but walk them during the off season or later season. For example, the Camino Portuguese is quieter in October. Or, take one of the lesser travelled routes such as the Camino de Levante or the Via De La Plata.

Some socialising/ some chill: For a more balanced Camino, I'd recommend the Camino del Norte.

Especially if you're doing this in the Summer, you can expect a laid back atmosphere, but with enough Pilgrims to get in some socialising.

Party Party Party: If you're looking to socialise and find like-minded travellers who are willing to burn the candle at both ends, then I'd recommend the Camino Frances. The French route has the highest number of Pilgrims, the most Albergues and more bars and restaurants than the others. Party On!

Are you craving a unique experience?

The path unknown: Perhaps you're looking for something totally unique? A road less travelled? The Camino de Levante stretches for over 1000km from the East of Spain (Valencia) all the way to Santiago. I'm yet to meet anyone who has taken this route! Another option is to take the Camino Invierno (The Winter Route!) Less than 1000 pilgrims use this route every year. It follows the Camino Frances, but cutting off particular areas that would be too difficult to cross in the Winter.

A bit unique: If you want something a bit different, but still easy to navigate, then I'd suggest either the Camino Portuguese or the Camino Del Norte. Both are popular and established routes, but not completely crowded (yet!)

Well trodden path: The Camino Frances might be the one of you if you want something established and easy to travel. Each year, this is the most popular route and it's very much set up for the numbers of travellers taking this way.

What scenery would you like?

Coastal: If windswept beaches, ocean views and cliff top walks are your thing, then the Camino Del Norte or the Camino Portuguese Coastal Route are the best ones for you! Both routes offer fantastic coastal scenery and the chance to enjoy an afternoon dip in the sea at the end of a hard days walking.

Mountain: The Camino Primitivo is one of the toughest camino routes owing to the undulating terrain. But this means you get incredible mountain scenery in return. The Camino Norte is also quite undulating and the views are really special.

Countryside: If you don't crave the ocean and you're looking for more consistent terrain, then the Camino Frances may be the one for you. This route winds inland across Spanish countryside, taking in wine regions and small towns and villages. The Portuguese inland route is also a good option.

What do you like to eat and drink?

White wine and seafood: The Camino del Norte journeys through Galicia, famed for both white wine and seafood!

Port and custard tarts: Say no more, if you're after a Pastel de Nata and a big glass of Port, then you should try the Camino Portuguese which kicks off in Porto.

Red wine and hearty fare: If this is you thing, then definitely try the Camino Frances, which travels through the Rioja wine region!

Which cities would you like to visit?

Bilbao: Want to visit the culinary capital of the Basque region? Try the Camino del Norte which takes in Bilbao and San Sebastian.

Oviedo: If you're looking to visit the capital of Asturias, then take the Camino Primitivo which winds through this great city.

Pamplona: Always wanted to visit the home of the famous Bull Run? Then take the Camino Frances which counts Pamplona as part of the route.

Madrid: There's even a Camino route running through the Spanish capital city. Give the Camino de Madrid a go – this route joins the Frances route just short of Leon.

CHAPTER FOUR: TRAINING FOR THE CAMINO

Once you've locked in which route you're going to take and you know how much time you have, you can start to think in more specific details about the distances you need to cover. Crucially, you can now start training.

Firstly, it's never too early to start training. The benefits of early and gradual training for the Camino, include giving your body longer to adjust to the demands you'll be placing on it and identifying any injuries that are likely to flare up.

Full disclosure, when we walked our first Camino de Santiago, we had reasonably high fitness levels. We could comfortably run 10km and would workout at least five times per week. I am also a fanatic yogi, and yoga instructor, so use that in my training too. But we didn't really walk long distances regularly, certainly not daily as we would need to do on the Camino. We did some training for our first Camino, but frankly, wish we had done more. Having now walked a few different long-distance paths, we've refined how we train and hope that the experience we have built up can help you prepare for the Camino too.

My training plan combines a mix of walking, strength training and yoga. This may not appeal to everyone. But I wanted to share it, because in my experience this combination is a great way to train to get stronger and more mobile before a long-distance hike like the Camino.

Walking

Walking has to be the main way to train for the Camino.

How much walking to do to prepare for a long-distance hike like the Camino de Santiago?

How much walking you need to do to prepare for the Camino de Santiago very much depends on your fitness levels and your prior experience. Additionally, much will depend on your goals for the Camino. There are plenty of people who do not plan to walk more than 10km to 15km per day on the Camino. Others aim to walk around 30km to 35km daily. The average that most pilgrims walk per day is between 20km and 25km each day. On this basis, the training suggestions below are written for the "average" walking goal of 20km to

25km.

Walking for a beginner

If you're completely new to hiking and you don't walk regularly, the most important thing is to start your training early! A good benchmark would be four to- six months prior to the Camino, but even earlier if you can.

A good starting distance to walk is 5km. We would suggest trying to walk at this distance a few times per week. After that, you can start to increase the distance gradually. The main focus should be to increase your pace a little each time you walk and walking regularly. A little each day can help.

Each week, we suggest introducing one longer walk. If you work Monday to Friday, the best time to do this might be on the weekend. If you want to make it more fun, maybe plan your walks around a visit to a coffee shop or pub- or bring a friend along! Most towns (at least in the UK) have some sort of ramblers' society or walking group - try reaching out to these groups to join some hikes too!

The best way (in our opinion) to introduce more walking into your life is to swap public transport or driving for walking whenever you can. It's surprising how many steps you can introduce each day if you choose to walk. Whether this is to the supermarket or on your daily commute, it can really add up and help to prepare you for regular walking on the Camino.

Introduce the backpack

If you plan to walk between 20km and 25km each day on the Camino, we suggest that you get one or two of these distances under your belt if you can. Ideally, try walking with your backpack with some weight too. Walking this distance at least once will give you the confidence to know you can do it! But also, help to identify any injuries that might flare up on the Camino so you can prepare for them.

Walking for more intermediate hikers

If you're a hiker with some experience, or a runner, you're likely to be able to walk at least 10km/ 15km comfortably. This was similar to our experience level before our first Camino. We could run 5km or 10km comfortably and walk 20km, with a little challenge. However, walking the Camino is different for two reasons.

Firstly, the Camino requires you to walk lengthy distances every day for a long period (an average of 30 days if you walk the full routes.) Secondly, you will always be carrying your backpack.

Therefore, for intermediate hikers we would recommend that these are your two focus areas during your walking training for the Camino (or the long-distance hike you are training for). Prior to the first Camino, we took some short camping trips over long-weekends. During these trips we aimed to walk at least 25km (which was our goal daily target for the Camino) and we carried weight similar to what we would carry on the Camino.

If you're regularly walking through the week, whether hiking or just getting from A to B, and you have a few practice walks under your belt - in our experience, this is enough! You don't need to walk 25km every day for a month to prepare for the Camino. There will be plenty of time to do that when you get there!

Equipment for training

Wherever you are in your journey prior to the Camino, we highly recommend trying to walk at least some distance with your backpack with a similar weight to what you will carry on the road. Additionally, it's great if you can wear the footwear (socks etc. too) that you plan to wear on the way, during your training. You'll quickly realise whether you're carrying too much weight on your back and whether there are any issues with footwear.

How to introduce mobility and strength training?

I am a certified yoga instructor, so I am a little biased, but I believe the best way to introduce strength and mobility training to prepare for hiking is through yoga. But I also regularly do pure strength training and there are benefits to including both in your Camino de Santiago training programme.

In addition to walking, as part of a training programme, there are clear benefits to introducing yoga and strength training into your training. These include:

- Creating more stamina and strength helping you to walk longer distances;
- Strength in your muscles helps to stabilise your joints, which reduces the risk of injury during hiking significantly;
- Increasing strength can help with carrying a heavy backpack for long periods of time;
- Improving the mobility of your body helps to prepare for daily movement undertaken on a multi-day hike;
- Yoga helps with mental preparation, which may benefit you during long distance hikes.

Which muscle groups are important for hiking?

Let's consider which muscle groups are most involved in hiking. The important muscle groups for hiking are:

- The glutes (the biggest muscle group in your butt)
- The hamstrings (the big muscle group at

the back of your thighs)
- The hip flexors (a group of muscles inside your core responsible for any flexion action at your hips i.e. lifting your leg up)
- The core (your abs and back muscles – the "corset" around your middle)

Many people think about hiking requiring strong legs, but few people realise the importance of the specific groups - the glutes and the hamstrings. Even fewer people consider how important their core and hip flexors are to hiking. Hip flexors are often overlooked because they are not visible!

Best strength exercises for hiking

These are my "go to" strength exercises ahead of walking a long-distance hike.

I include a combination of single leg exercises (asymmetric) and double leg (symmetrical). This is particularly important for hiking long distances because we can tend to "favour" one leg over the other. If you only train both legs at the same time, this allows one leg to do all the work and the other to become weaker. The long-term consequence of this can be injury on one side. Therefore, exercising both legs individually can help to keep the muscles strong on both sides and prevent injury.

For an additional challenge, perhaps nearer to your walk, start doing these exercises with your hiking backpack on.

Squats

Squats, and the dynamic alternative of squats (squat jumps), are a super training exercise for hiking.

Benefits: Glute and leg strength muscles, increases stability to assist with hiking.

Beginner Tips: Try to increase the number you do and how low you can go into the squat but maintain the posture.

Pistol Squats

Benefits: An asymmetric/ unilateral move that works each side individually to strengthen the legs and improve stability.

Beginner Tips: You can build this move up gradually, it is quite tricky. Don't go as low as is shown in this picture at first.

Lunges

Benefits: An asymmetric/ unilateral exercise that works each leg individually. Benefits stability in legs, which is needed when hiking.

Beginner Tips: Try static lunges (pulsing up and down in the lunge position) before you progress to forward or reverse lunges.

Mini-Band Walks

Mini-band walks (also called monster walks) are an exercise that many physios recommend for anyone with weak glute muscles. In this exercise, you use an exercise band around your ankles and walk forward one step at a time.

Benefits: Isolates the glutes to strengthen them.

Beginner Tips: The band needs to be tight to be effective.

Plank variants

There are several variants to the plank pose that can help strength training for hiking. I normally introduce a high plank and low plank (forearms on the mat) hold into my regimes. I also use plank shoulder taps in my training - this is where you tap your right hand to your left shoulder (and vice versa), whilst maintaining your posture in the position.

Benefits: Core strength and stability. Shoulder strength and stability (if using shoulder taps).

Beginner Tips: Hold this pose for less time and build up to holding it for longer. Try 20 shoulder taps, and gradually increase the number.

Best yoga poses to train for hiking

Here are the best yoga poses that you can incorporate into your long-distance hiking training plan. You can sequence these into a short yoga flow or treat them as separate poses.

High Lunge

Benefits: Leg and glute strengthening and excellent for stabilising hips and knees whilst legs are active.

Beginner Tips: Keep the back leg straight and bend into the front knee as far as possible. You are aiming for a right angle between your shin and thigh of the front leg, with the thigh parallel to the floor.

Hand to toe pose

Benefits: This standing pose helps balance and body awareness. It also strengthens the standing and lifted leg, from the glutes through to the ankles.

Beginner Tips: There are two variants to this pose, one with your leg out in front of your body and one with your leg to the side. It' s OK if you can't straighten your leg fully in this pose at first. Try this with a bent knee. Or, if you can't reach your toes you can just hold your knee.

Tree pose

Benefits: This pose improves your balance as well as focus. The standing leg is active and engaged, creating strength in the leg and glute muscles.

Beginner Tips: The foot of the bent leg can rest

against the calf, if it doesn't reach the thigh. But be careful not to put your foot directly onto your knee of the standing leg.

Boat pose

Benefits: This pose is great for core strength and to strengthen the hip flexors.

Beginner Tips: You can do this pose with bent or straight legs. You can also hold onto your thighs to make it easier too.

Plank pose

Benefits: Core strength and stability.

Beginner Tips: Hold this for small amounts of time at first. Keep the core engaged and stop your hips from dropping down towards the floor.

Flexibility and Mobility

The less mobile your skeletal frame and muscles are, the more likely you are to pick up injuries. A few months before taking on the Camino, it can be a really good idea to start introducing some yoga into your exercise regime. Failing that, some easy daily stretching could go a long way to increasing your flexibility before you walk.

CHAPTER FIVE: BUDGETING FOR THE CAMINO DE SANTIAGO

How much does it cost to walk the Camino de Santiago?

The next area that you may want to consider with regards to starting to prepare for the Camino de Santiago, is budget.

Upfront costs before the Camino de Santiago

You are likely to have a small amount of upfront costs when walking the Camino de Santiago. We estimated that our travel costs and equipment costs were around 5% of our overall spend on the Camino. This included new trainers, backpacks, and clothing. However, our flight costs were limited as we were flying from the UK to France and returning from Spain. For anyone travelling from the USA or Australia the costs for travel will be higher.

Daily budget for the Camino de Santiago

In general, we think that there are ways to walk the Camino de Santiago on pretty much any budget. There are some tips below for walking the Camino on a shoestring budget if you choose to do this. However, we have also set out the average daily budget - based on prices in 2022 on the main routes (Portuguese, French and North Route.)

We have based this on anyone walking the Camino de Santiago independently and carrying their own bags, rather than as part of a tour or with luggage transfer costs.

Accommodation costs

For a bed in a dorm, the average Municipal Albergue is around 10 Euros (but some cost less) with Private Albergues rising to between 15 and 20 Euros. Private rooms will cost more, ranging between 25 and 50 Euros.

Food and drink costs

- Menu Del Dia (3 courses with a drink) will range from 10 to 20 Euros
- A main course will range from 6 to 12 Euros
- A baguette in a supermarket will range from 50 Cents to 1 Euro
- A pack of pasta will cost around 1.50

Euros
- A pastry in a bakery will cost between 1 and 1.50 Euros
- Coffee will cost between 1.20 and 2 Euros (but 2 would seem pricey!)
- A glass of house wine will cost between 1.50 and 2.50 Euros
- A beer will cost between 1.50 and 2 Euros
- An average daily budget based on eating out once a day, staying in private Albergues and drinking wine and beer: Approx 40 Euros

An average daily budget based on cooking and packing lunch, staying in Municipal Albergues and drinking less: **Approx 20 Euros**

Top tips for walking the Camino de Santiago on a budget

- Stay in Municipal and Donativo Albergues where you can.
- Some Albergue's have breakfast included in the rate or offered very cheaply (2 euros approx).
- Pick Albergues that have communal dinners – these tend to be cheaper than eating out in a restaurant.
- Shop in the supermarket for your breakfasts and lunches, prepare this in advance the night before and take it with you. Alternatively, a fresh baguette in a

bakery can be really cheap.
- Find Albergues with kitchens so that you can cook in the evenings. If you buy a bag of pasta, you could take some with you for future evening meals. You could also find a friend in the Albergue willing to split a meal, sometimes it can be cheaper to cook for two.
- Look out for Pilgrim deals in restaurants but be aware that sometimes they are a bit of a false economy.
- Drinks out in Spain and Portugal area quite cheap but stick to local beer or wine if you want to save money. Soft drinks in bars are surprisingly expensive comparatively.

CHAPTER SIX: PACKING FOR THE CAMINO DE SANTIAGO

In the final run up to walking the Camino, you'll need to start thinking about packing. If you get this right, you'll have a much smoother journey. Get in wrong, and it can be a nightmare!

What size backpack do you need for the Camino de Santiago?

Most people walking a long-distance hike such as the Camino de Santiago will carry a backpack of between 30 and 40 litres. This should be sufficient to carry all of your essentials including a sleeping bag, if you decide to take one.

If you're planning to walk every day, please do NOT take a bag any bigger than 40L. I promise, you will regret it if you do! I take a 30L bag and my partner takes 40L. I have seen people walking the Camino with far bigger bags, sometimes 60L. The problem with taking such a large bag, is that you'll be tempted to fill it. If you keep your bag small, it is much more of a challenge to pack too much.

How much should your backpack weigh on the Camino de Santiago?

As a guide, your backpack for walking on the Camino de Santiago should not weigh more than 10% of your body weight. So, if you weigh 80kg, the backpack should weigh no more than 8kg.

There may be exceptions, if for example you are very strong or used to carrying weight whilst exercising. However, it's important to remember that you are likely to be walking long distances every day on the Camino de Santiago. Any extra weight on your back is likely to put unnecessary strain on your body and could lead to injury, or at least discomfort.

And remember, when you weigh your bag before you go, weigh it with your water bottle filled. Your daily water allowance will add significant weight.

Best backpacks for the Camino de Santiago 2023:

There are a few important things to look for when you are trying to find your backpack for the Camino de Santiago:

- Correct fit - backpacks come in different

sizes to suit different heights, pick the correct one and find a backpack with adjustable straps
- Backpack weight - check the weight of your pack when it is empty
- Backpack size - look for something between 30 and 40 litres that you can also carry onto an airplane
- Pockets and sections - look for a bag with hip compartments, side pockets and other zipped sections
- Hip and chest straps - ensure that your backpack has hip and chest straps to take the weight off your shoulders
- Finally, don't forget to try it before you walk the Camino and return it if it doesn't feel right. And of course, don't forget to train with the backpack on.

Here are five of our favourite backpacks for the Camino de Santiago in 2023:

1. Best for women – Osprey Sirrus 34 Women's Hiking Backpack
2. Best for petite women – Osprey Tempest 30 – available in Small Size
3. Most stylish backpack – Fjällräven Kaipak 38 Backpack 55 cm
4. Best for men – Osprey Talon 33 litre
5. Best unisex option – Deuter Unisex Futura Pro 36 Backpack

How to pack your backpack for the Camino de Santiago

It may sound silly, but packing your backpack efficiently can make your trip much easier.

Here are our top tips:

Firstly, it is extremely helpful to separate the items in your backpack so that you can get quick access to anything you need when you arrive at your hostel. This would include your toiletries, your power cables, trek towel, and anything you need for sleeping. You can use a carrier bag to separate everything or use packing cubes. Having a separate toiletries bag can also speed things up when you need to get access to your toiletries and jump in the shower.

Secondly, try to keep your dirty clothes and walking clothes separate to your fresh evening clothes. When walking every day, especially in the summer, your walking clothes can get quite pungent!

Next, think about what you might need to get access to during your walk. Look for a backpack with handy pockets for these items. You may want somewhere to stash your phone, sunscreen, lip balm and anything else you want during the walk. Finally, I love using a water platypus which slots into a pocket at the back of my bag. This means I can access my water as I walk.

Best footwear for the Camino de Santiago

In our experience, trail shoes are the best footwear for the Camino de Santiago. The majority of the routes are on road, footpaths and trails. Although there are some hill climbs, the walking surfaces are rarely uneven and therefore walking boots are not really required.

We have recently started wearing Hoka trail running shoes and we were really delighted with our purchases. Hoka uses innovative technology to create shoes that are really supportive. These can be great for anyone with injuries, particularly if you normally experience foot pain when walking long distances.

The trail shoes are also a little water resistant and have grips that are ideal for walking on footpaths, including muddy surfaces. We have previously tried New Balance shoes and Nike running shoes for long walks, but we feel that Hoka were the best we've tried for long distance hiking like the Camino.

If you are injury free, don't suffer from ankle issues etc, and you are walking any of the Camino de Santiago routes in summer, you do not need hiking boots. I saw many pilgrims being forced to carry their heavy boots on their backs when they had come to this realisation. In the Summer it is too hot and unnecessary to be wearing anything other than trainers, sandals or light weight hiking shoes. For the Primitivo, you may want hiking boots with more ankle support. If you're walking in spring, autumn or winter (eek), then make sure your footwear is waterproof. If you get trainers wet, it can be difficult to dry them as most Albergues do not have heaters or anywhere to dry shoes. After a few days of getting damp, they will start to stink!

Whatever you choose, try them on a couple of long hikes before you take them with you! I cannot emphasise this enough. After 20km, you will quickly identify whether the shoes are Camino ready or not and far better to this before you get on the trails!

Two Words –Pop Socks! A friend gave me this tip before I left the UK and I could not be more grateful. Although I did get a couple of blisters towards the end of the Camino, I managed about 20 days of blister free glee after opting to wear a pop sock under my hiking sock. I passed this tip on to loads of fellow pilgrims and they also loved it. A veritable Pop Sock pyramid scheme.

I highly recommend a lightweight pair of flip flops, for the evenings. There is no greater feeling than removing your hiking shoes at the end of a long day and sliding on some flops. *Joyful music*. You could also take a lightweight pair of canvas shoes in cooler months.

Clothing

For men and women, the clothing required is really similar. Gone are the days of Pilgrim's wearing cloaks and strange hats, now it's all about light weight, quick dry sports clothing.

Walking Clothes

- Shorts
- Trousers (Many people pack the hiking trousers that transform into shorts – if this is your jam, then go for it. I tend to pack leggings and separate shorts)
- Quick Dry Tops
- Long Sleeved Top or Jumper
- Poncho or Waterproof Jacket
- Hat
- Underwear
- Socks
- Sports Bra (Ladies)
- Bikini or swimwear (Ladies, a bikini top could double as a bra for the evening)

For walking, I opted for two of everything. Shorts, sports bras, t shirts, shorts and socks. This worked, as I could wash my clothing in the evening and hang it to my bag to dry the next day. However, if you're not walking in the summer, you might limit to one of each item as it will be difficult to wash and dry clothes as frequently (and it's likely you won't get as sweaty.)

If you're walking in colder months, then a woollen hat (rather than a sun hat), gloves, a jacket and extra warm layers should be considered.

Evening Clothes

When you're not walking, you will want a clean change of clothes for the evening. Things that can work well are:

- Lightweight trousers
- T shirts
- Denim shorts (if not too heavy)
- A lightweight dress
- A light shirt

Nobody is dressed smartly in the evening when walking the Camino. But you might want something presentable if you're planning to eat out in the evening.

Don't forget pyjamas, or something you can comfortably wear in a communal room in an Albergue.

Toiletries

This is where things get tricky. If, like me, you are used to having an abundance of toiletries, the Camino will challenge you. Toiletries are totally personal, but here are my top tips (this is mainly for ladies!)

- All in one soap – yup, it's a thing. You can get it on Amazon. Soap that washes you, your hair and your clothing. It's marvellous. Pack it in a plastic zip lock bag (not a heavy soap dish!)
- Sachets of Conditioner OR a leave in conditioner – a bottle of conditioner may be too heavy, but a few sachets of conditioner or an intensive hair mask are easier to carry.
- For ladies – a mooncup – carrying tampax or sanitary towels is heavy, a mooncup is not. I'd also recommend this for ease as sometimes the toilets on the trail are infrequent.
- Moisturiser for body and face – an all in one moisturiser will save space and weight in your bag, for me this as non-negotiable especially to moisturise my feet.
- Vaseline – can be used as lip balm, moisturiser and even make up remover at a push
- Suncream – goes without saying. I find a spray easier to use on the trails and lighter to carry too.
- Bug Spray – during the night, you won't be in control of whether windows or doors are open. If you don't want to get bitten then I'd suggest taking a small spray.

- A small medical kit – allergy tablets, Ibuprofen, rehydration sachets and blister plasters.
- A little makeup for the evening – mascara and a lip balm that also acts as a cheek tint is very helpful
- Cleansing wipes – a lightweight packet of cleansing wipes
- Deodorant – something under 100ml and lightweight
- Toothpaste and toothbrush

Electronics

You won't always be able to get access to a plug in your Albergue, so I would highly recommend taking a spare battery pack for charging your phone on the go. A long charging cable can be handy too, as you may not always have a plug near to your bed. I also took wireless headphones – this may not be for everyone, but I found these invaluable for listening to podcasts during long days on the trails and for blocking out noise at night in the Albergue.

Handy Bits and Pieces

As well as clothes and toiletries, there are a few really handy items that you could consider taking along.

- A deck of cards – useful for socialising in the evenings.

- Trek towel – you'll need a trek towel as most Albergue's will not give you towels. Something lightweight and quick dry is perfect.
- A sleeping bag or sleeping sheet – not always necessary, but it's more comfortable to have a sleeping bag, sleeping bag line or sleeping sheet to use in bunk beds. It feels way more hygienic. In summer, a sleeping bag will be too much, but a sheet is perfect. If you're on a budget, you could just take a cheap sheet (you could even sew it to make a sheet bag.)
- Pegs - something strong to attach clothing to your bag when it's drying and to hang clothes on the line at the Albergue.
- Small plastic bags – one for your dirty clothing and some smaller ones just in case!
- Toilet paper – I'm not suggesting you pack this with you, but it's useful to put a few sheets in your bag as you leave the Albergue in the morning. Sometimes, you will have to have a nature wee. I also take Zip Lock bags, which could be come in handy to put used toilet paper in. Say no more.
- Ear plugs and eye mask – Albergues are noisy, and lights go on and off at different times as everyone is on a different

schedule.
- Blister Plasters – of course you can buy these in the different towns along the Camino, but if you have a favourite brand (Compeed for me!) then it's worth having them handy.
- Ibuprofen – again you can buy these easily, but I like to have some in my bag just in case.
- Bottle opener – most wine in Spain has a cork not a screw top. If you're a wine drinker, then a bottle opener can be useful.
- Waterproof bag cover – it will rain and you want to be able to cover your bag quickly to keep things dry.
- Albergue Bag - You can use packing cubes (fancy) or just a plastic bag, but I recommend having a bag inside your backpack with everything you need when you get to the Albergue, such as your towel, your Pjs and your phone charger.
- Canvas Bag of Bum Bag (Fanny Pack) - In an evening, you will want to leave your backpack in the Albergue if you're going out. A bum bag or just a canvas shoulder bag is perfect to pop a few items in when you head out.
- A travel adaptor is also required unless you already have European plugs. Or, if you just have your phone charger with you, you can buy a European plug for that.

- A water receptacle – either a large bottle or a water platypus
- A pen and small notebook – if you like to keep a journal in the evening.

CHAPTER SEVEN: FREQUENTLY ASKED QUESTIONS

In this chapter, I will cover some of the most Frequently Asked Questions that people tend to have before walking the Camino de Santiago for the first time.

Is the Camino de Santiago a religious walk?

The Camino de Santiago is a modern-day long-distance trail that has historic origins. It is called The Way of St James as it is believed that the remains of Saint James, an important Saint in Catholicism, are in Santiago. Therefore, many Catholics in the 10th and 11th centuries would walk the Camino to Santiago for the purpose of religious pilgrimage.

In short, the Camino de Santiago is a walk with religious origins and taking a pilgrimage to

Santiago is an important Catholic tradition.

Do you have to be religious to walk the Camino?

Whilst the Camino de Santiago is historically a religious pilgrimage it is not exclusively for religious people or Catholics today. Many people walk the Camino (178,912 in 2021 and 438,683 in 2022). This includes some who self-declare as religious and others who do not. There are many people of all faiths who walk the Camino de Santiago, including people with faith other than Catholic or Christian.

According to statistics recorded by the Pilgrim's Office in Santiago, 36.37% of individuals completing the Camino de Santiago in 2021 declared that they did so for solely religious reasons. This compares to 20.45% who sited "non-religious" motivation and a majority of 43.2% who claimed to complete the Camino for "religious and other" reasons.

If you choose to walk the Camino de Santiago and you are not religious, you should be able to respect the fact that many people walking the Camino de Santiago will be religious. The path has a religious history associated with it and many choose to walk the path to this day for religious reasons. You will meet Christian and Catholic people and should expect this and be able to respectfully participate alongside religious people.

As you walk the Camino, you will also can visit many churches and cathedrals. You can also choose to stay in monasteries and convents. When you stay at these places you will be invited to attend mass or other ceremonies. However, these are all optional experiences during the Camino.

Is there WiFi on the Camino de Santiago?

Walking the Camino de Santiago is one of life's s big adventures and so much fun, especially if it's your first time walking the Camino. Whilst it may feel like you're venturing into paths new, you don't have to worry that you will be straying too far from civilisation - you will have access to WiFi.

There is WiFi at various stages along the Camino on all of the routes. 99% of albergues have WiFi that is available either in the communal areas or in the dorm rooms.

In addition, most cafes and restaurants have WiFi and will give you the access code as long as you're a customer. Not all of them do, but many in bigger towns will.

Some people think that it's a shame that it is now so easy to access WiFi on the Camino! I can see what they mean. But remember, it is a choice as to whether you connect. You can always take the time to Digital Detox as you walk!

Are there places to charge your phone on the

Camino de Santiago?

Alas, you will not go without phone battery on the Camino de Santiago. But your ability to charge your phone regularly will depend on the accommodation that you choose.

In guesthouses and up-market private Albergues you will invariably have a plug socket by your bed. Most bunk beds in private Albergues have an individual socket. However, in municipal Albergues you often won't have one by your bed and may have to share with others in the hostel. Therefore, you can't be guaranteed to get a socket when you need it.

We always recommend packing a battery pack, and a long phone cable, just in case you can't get to a socket, or you need to use one that is a little distance away. Don't forget a travel adaptor too if you're from outside of Europe.

Is there phone signal on the Camino de Santiago?

Although you will be in parts of rural Spain, France or Portugal, you will have phone signal on the Camino de Santiago. There was one area of the Camino North route that we had limited signal for one day of walking, but the for the rest you will most likely have it (depending on your network.)

If you're doing a route that takes around a month, it can be sensible to buy a local SIM card if you want to be able to access your phone regularly.

But don't forget that there is WiFi available on the Camino.

Do I need to speak Spanish on the Camino?

The Camino de Santiago is in Spain and the largest proportion of people walking the Camino each year are from Spain. Therefore, the main language is Spanish. However, significant numbers are from Germany, Italy, the UK, and the USA and many from elsewhere around the world. Therefore, not everyone walking the Camino can speak Spanish.

English is widely spoken across Spain, although not everybody has high proficiency levels. This can be the case in rural areas of Spain that you may walk through on the Camino. However, most people who work in the tourist industry in B&Bs, hotel and large restaurants and bars, especially in bigger cities and towns, will speak some English (or other languages to Spanish.)

During the three Caminos that we walked, we met only one or two Pilgrims who spoke only Spanish and no English, but language barriers have never proved to be an issue when socialising with other pilgrims on the Camino.

It is absolutely not vital to speak Spanish if you walk the Camino. But learning a few phrases can go a long way and may make you feel more confident as you navigate your Camino adventure.

Helpful Spanish phrases for walking the Camino

There are a few phrases or words that you could learn in Spanish that may make your Camino experience a little smoother. For example, when booking Albergues (see below), ordering food or communicating with locals. When you visit a restaurant or cafe or arrange accommodation, these are the most likely times when it may be helpful to speak a little Spanish.

Here are some Spanish phrases that may come in handy on the Camino:

Hello: Hola
Good bye: Adiós
Please: Por favor
Thank you: Gracias
I am from England/ USA: Soy de Inglaterra/ Soy de estados unidos
Do you speak English: ¿Hablas inglés?
Do you have a bed for tomorrow/ today: ¿Tienes una cama para mañana?/ ¿Tienes una cama para hoy?
Can I make a reservation for tonight: ¿Puedo hacer una reserva para esta noche?
One beer: Una Cerveza
One coffee with milk and one coffee without milk: Un café con leche y un café sin leche (or cafe solo)
White wine/ Red wine: Vino blanco/ vino tinto
More drinks/ another round: más bebidas/ Otra ronda

I would like a sandwich: Me gustaría un bocadillo
Do you have a menu of the day: ¿Tienes un menú del día?
Where is the hotel: Dónde está el hotel
Do you have a stamp: ¿Tienes un sello?
I am walking the Camino: Estoy caminando el camino
How are you: Cómo estás
Very well: muy bien

Don't forget to follow the key phrases with please"Por favor"as needed.

Those who know more of the language than us may point out that there are different ways to say "you" in Spanish, including a formal way. You may use this formal version of you when addressing somebody you have not met or spoken to before, or perhaps an elder. Therefore, if you are calling a new Albergue and you haven't spoken to them before, you could use the formal version. For example "Tiene usted una cama para manana?" or "Tiene usted un menu del dia?" However, in our experience of travelling in Spain, most people will understand what you mean and won't be offended if you get the wrong"you" and use the informal version.

Remember, that in Spain, there are also different dialects. For example, in Galicia, Galician is spoken rather than Spanish. In the Basque country (on the North Route), Basque is spoken rather than

Spanish too. And of course, if you walk the Portuguese route, expect to find people speaking Portuguese there!

How to book Albergues on the Camino?

One of the occasions when it may be helpful to speak Spanish on the Camino is if you book an Albergue. You don't always need to book Albergues in advance, but there are times when booking on the day, or the night before, can be helpful.

Many Albergues are now available to book online. But for smaller and municipal, or traditional, Albergues you will not be able to book online. The best way to book many Albergues on the day is to call them on the phone.

Whilst many Albergue managers will speak English, or other languages in addition to Spanish, some may not. Therefore, it can be helpful to speak a little Spanish to be able to make a reservation for an Albergue if you need to.

If you can learn to ask to make a reservation in Spanish, this will go a long way on the Camino. We do not speak much Spanish at all, but were able to learn to say "¿Tienes una cama para mañana?" (Do you have a bed for tomorrow) in a clear enough accent to be understood on the phone!

What is a Camino de Santiago credential?

A "credential" is essentially a passport that

identifies you as a pilgrim. It is normally in the form of a paper or cardboard concertina booklet. It is believed that the first pilgrims walking the Camino had a similar document, which is where the modern-day credential has originated from.

When you are given the booklet, it will be blank and you can complete your personal details, such as name, date of birth and nationality. Inside the booklet there are normally 32 small squares. The squares are there so that you can collect ink stamps as you travel along the Camino.

The credential not only gives you access to special hostels that are reserved only for pilgrims walking the Camino, but it may also entitle you to discounted menu options at restaurants and discounts at museums, such as the Pilgrim Museum in Santiago de Compostela. Crucially, the credential will be used to evidence your walk when you arrive in Santiago. This enables you get to get your certificate and your Compostela.

Where can I get a Camino credential from?

You can get a Camino credential at all the major start points for the main Camino routes.

For the North Route you can get a Camino credential in Irun at the municipal Albergue. You may also be able to find one at the cathedral or the police station in Irun, but the Albergue opens late so this is your best bet.

For the Portuguese Route, you can get a Camino credential in the Cathedral in Porto. This is a very organised and quick process but watch out for opening hours (0900 to 1730) if you are planning to head off early in the morning then you may need to get the credential the night before.

For the French Route, you can get a Camino credential easily in St. Jean Pied de Port at the official Pilgrim's Office, details here.

The credential will cost around 1 to 2 Euros or be provided on a donation basis.

You will also find that many Albergues near to the last 100km before Santiago sell Camino credentials. They can also be found at Albergues or churches near to the main start towns.

How to use the Camino credential?

The credential is a form of "passport" therefore you can use this every time you check into an Albergue to make it clear that you are pilgrim walking or cycling the Camino.

At each Albergue you will be able to get a "stamp" (called a sello in Spanish), in your credential booklet. It's fun to collect these stamps as many of them are great designs and colourful. But not only that, you can use the dated stamps to prove where you have walked at the end of your journey.

It's important that if you want to get the Compostela certificate in Santiago that you get stamps twice per day for the last 100km of your walk into Santiago. This is the last 200km of your cycle if you're on a bike.) This is to certify that you have indeed walked the last bit into Santiago and haven't cheated in some way.

Aside from Albergues, you can get stamps in churches, cathedrals and often at bars and restaurants on the Camino route.

The credential may also get you access to museums in Santiago, the mass at Santiago Cathedral and discounts in restaurants that sell "pilgrim menus." Although in reality most restaurants will not ask for proof as it will be pretty obvious that you're travelling on the Camino! The backpack, shell and faint stench may be a dead giveaway.

How do I get a certificate for the Camino?

To get a certificate for the Camino, you must attend the Pilgrims Office in Santiago. This is not in the cathedral but is very close. You must take your Camino credential with you and be sure to register.

How do I register for the Camino?

You can register online when you start the Camino. If you miss registering at the start don't worry. You don't have to register at the start, indeed you don't need to register at all if you don't want to. You can still get your Camino credential booklet if you don't register. But if you don't register then your walk will not be logged at the Pilgrim's Office in Santiago. This will mean that you cannot get the certificate.

If you walk the Portuguese route, you might be given a QR code on your credential to register online. For other routes, you can register for the Camino de Santiago through the official Pilgrim's website.

Do you need a sleeping bag for the Camino de Santiago?

This was something that we really didn't know the answer to during our first time walking the Camino de Santiago. Walking the Camino is not the same as walking a rough trail, the infrastructure on the Camino is really good with Albergues set up just for Pilgrims. Nonetheless, it's important as part of your preparation to consider what equipment you need carefully.

If you plan to stay in an albergue dormitory room, you will invariably be sleeping on a bunk bed. The bunk beds will vary from luxurious, like in some of our favourite Albergues on the Camino Portuguese, to darn right basic. Many municipal albergues have bunk beds with old mattresses.

Most tend to provide you with a plastic disposable sheet that you can put over the mattress, as well as a plastic disposable pillowcase.

In our experience, guest houses, pensions or basic hotels will all have sheets and blankets. If you're planning to stay in these and not in albergues, then you won't need a sleeping bag.

If the idea of sleeping under a heavy woollen blanket that hasn't been washed frequently freaks you out – then yes, you will need a sleeping bag or a sleep sheet on the Camino.

In theory, you could probably go without. Most Albergues have blankets, but it doesn't feel very pleasant to have this as your only option if it's very hot in the night, or if you don't like the idea of using a blanket that somebody else has used the night before.

If you're not planning to stay in Albergues, then I would suggest you do not need a sleeping bag.

Do albergues have blankets on the Camino?

Albergues on the Camino do mostly tend to have blankets. You will either be provided with a blanket on your bed, or you will be able to find one in a cupboard or ask the hostel manager. On one or two occasions during the three times we have walked the Camino, we have been told that we need to pay a small fee (1 Euro) to borrow a blanket or a duvet.

The blankets tend to be very thick woollen blankets. If you are walking the Camino in the off-season, or you get cold in the night, then you might use this blanket. But, if you are walking during the summer, it is most likely going to feel far too hot to use the blanket.

Do you need hiking poles for the Camino de Santiago?

Are hiking poles necessary for the Camino? It's a completely personal choice. Whether or not you need hiking poles will depend on which route you are walking and the terrain, your walking experience and your body! For some people, hiking poles will provide huge benefit. For others, they are not necessary and will just feel like extra weight on your back.

What are the advantages of using hiking poles?

There are three main advantages to using hiking poles:

1// Hiking poles can help your balance and stability

Having the two poles to lean on can help you maintain balance and stability. This is particularly useful if you're walking up or down slippery or difficult terrain. There are some steep ascents and descents on the Camino Norte and the Camino

Primitivo too, but other Camino routes are flatter and you may not find your balance is challenged enough to warrant the use of hiking poles.

2// Hiking poles can take pressure of your lower body

The joints and muscles in your legs can take a battering when you're walking long distances every day on the Camino. Using hiking poles can take pressure off your lower body. If you have lower body injuries, then hiking poles could be of benefit to you.

3// Hiking poles can help to maintain pace and rhythm

A bit like skiing with poles, hiking poles can help you find a nice rhythm. In turn, this can also help to maintain or increase your pace of walking.

What are the disadvantages of using hiking poles?

The main disadvantage of using hiking poles is that you will have to carry them! Hiking poles are extra weight to carry when you're not using them, including on the plane. As noted below, you will also have to put them in the hold on the plane, which can be costly.

The second disadvantage of using hiking poles on the Camino, is that it's an extra thing to keep an eye on. This may sound silly, but we really enjoy the minimalism of hiking with less. This is the main reason we don't use poles, because it just feels like something else to think about! Plus, people frequently leave them behind in albergues or restaurants and have to retrace their steps to find them!

On the Camino, particularly the North Route, there can be a lot of walking on road and walking through towns. Hiking poles don't really provide much benefit on this sort of terrain.

There is some research suggesting that using hiking poles can take up more energy than not using them. I don't know how accurate this is, but there seems to be some logic to the argument, given that using hiking poles requires you to use your arms more.

Finally, you may find yourself at the end of quite a few (gentle and good natured) jokes about hiking poles if you use them.

How much do hiking poles cost?

There is a range of hiking poles on the market at various price points.

A budget set of hiking poles can be found for around £25. Mid-range hiking poles retail at £60 ish. More expensive carbon fibre poles are in the region of about £150.

How much do hiking poles weigh?

The weight of hiking poles will depend on what type of pole you choose as well as the size of the poles. Carbon fibre poles are likely to weigh a little less than aluminium.

Budget aluminium poles are likely to weigh about 250g, whereas carbon fibre are more like 200g.

Can you use just one hiking pole?

The original pilgrims walking the Camino likely walked with just one "staff", which is a bit like a modern-day hiking pole. You could use just one hiking pole to walk the Camino. The advantages of this would be that one pole is less weight to carry than two. If you have an injury or weakness on one side, then there are indications that one pole could help.

Using one hiking pole will likely provide a bit of stability and may be beneficial particularly if you're hiking down or up difficult terrain. But you won't reap the same benefits that you would by using two poles.

Can you take hiking poles on the plane?

Yes, you can take hiking poles on the plane. But you cannot take them in your hand luggage into the cabin. Most airlines specify that hiking or climbing poles must go into the hold. If you're just travelling with a hiking backpack and poles, this might be tricky as you may not wish to put your backpack (your Camino treasure) into the hold.

Where to buy hiking poles for the Camino in Spain?

If you decide not to take them on the plane, you could buy them when you arrive in Spain to start the Camino. There are a few options.

Either, find a trekking store in Irun, Porto, Oviedo, Saint Jean Pied de Port or wherever you are starting. There are several Decathlon stores in Spain, France and Portugal. This store is always a great bet if you're looking for any sort of hiking gear, including poles. Check the latest Decathlon locations, but at time of writing there is one on the outskirts of Porto and Irun. Stores can also be found at various points on the route, including Gijon on the North Route.

Another option is to order them on Amazon to an Amazon Hub locker near to the start point of the Camino. We have done this many times if we need something overseas and can't get it onto the plane. It can work out to be much cheaper than paying for luggage on a plane.

SECTION TWO: WALKING THE CAMINO

"Travel is glamorous only in retrospect." – Paul Theroux

CHAPTER EIGHT: ALBERGUE GUIDE

Albergues are quite a unique Camino de Santiago experience. This chapter will cover all that you need to know about booking, checking in and thriving in the Albergue environment.

Firstly, a bit more detail on Albergues. What is an Albergue?

An Albergue is a hostel, normally with dormitories, that are often exclusively for Pilgrims walking the Camino. There are generally two types – Municipal and Private. Municipal are often cheaper and more basic, designed to make the Camino accessible for all. Private Albergues tend to have better facilities as they tend to be run for profit. There are also Donativo Albergues (donate what you can) which are privately run too. In recent years, Donativo Albergues are harder to find. Most have found that this model is increasingly difficult to run and often they are completely reliant on Pilgrims making donations and volunteers running the Albergues. Trends indicate that Private Albergues are now dominating the market, particularly those with "luxury" facilities, like nice linen and towels and even swimming pools.

Choosing Albergues

You'll find when walking the Camino that some towns and villages only have one Albergue and you won't have a choice. There are often Pensions or cheap hotels in the same area, but not always.

We are huge fans of the Buen Camino app, which we have used again and again to plan our route and find Albergues. There are exceptions, but generally the Albergue directory on this app is really up to date and comprehensive.

If you have a choice between Albergues, you can look at Pilgrim review scores or google photos to check them out in advance. You may also want to consider whether you want a kitchen to cook and whether you want somewhere with outdoor or communal space, or you could opt for somewhere more central if that's important to you.

We would also advise checking out pictures of the bunk beds. The sleep set up can be vastly different in Albergues. Some have rickety old bunk beds and frankly you don't stand much chance of a decent sleep in that environment. Others have curtains to provide privacy, which we find conducive to a good night's sleep.

We would also recommend staying flexible and open minded. We've stayed at many Albergues that we didn't expect to like but turned out to be fantastic experiences. And if you stay flexible about where you're going, and meet friends along the way, then you choose to go to the same Albergue together.

Booking

For some private Albergues, you can now book on Booking.com. But remember, if you do this and your plans change, you may not be able to cancel. For others, you could call the Albergue on the day to secure a reservation or email them. Normally, the private Albergues will allow a reservation this way but will give you a set arrival time and will give up your bed if you're too late. Municipal Albergues will rarely take reservations and normally you must be there between 1300 and 1500 to wait for opening. Times vary between Albergue so check this on the app or online.

You do not always have to book. If you're someone who likes to plan and the idea of finding an Albergue on the day is too stressful, then go ahead and book. But if you want to maintain an air of spontaneity, then in some situations you will be fine without a reservation. Just look out for bottle necks on the route (towns that every Pilgrim will have to stop in that day) and keep an eye on whether booking is required in that case.

Arriving

Arrival into an Albergue is quite straightforward and similar to checking into a hostel. You'll have to show your passport or ID card and your Pilgrim credential. Some Albergues only take cash, so always have this to hand when checking in unless you're sure that they accept card.

You may be assigned a bunk bed, or you might be given the choice. If you know you'll be up early or going to bed late, it can be sensible to choose a bed near the door. But if you're a light sleeper, then pick one well away! Top bunks tend to be hotter and the steps can be difficult to climb, so ask for a bottom bunk if you know this could be an issue for you.

You'll probably need to wash your clothes, most Albergues have dedicated laundry areas for this and somewhere to hang clothes. We would recommend locating the laundry area quickly and getting your laundry washed and hanging to maximise drying time (but remember, you can peg it to your bag to dry the next day if needed).

Lastly, suss out the plug points on arrival. You may not have one in your bunk so if you've got items that need to be changed it can be sensible to get in there early.

Etiquette

There are some quite simple, but unspoken rules, to be aware of in Albergues. Apart from the obvious hygiene and social etiquette, the main things to do are:

- Keep your hiking shoes/boots out of the dorms
- Keep noise to an absolute minimum through the night
- If lights are out in the dorm, do not turn them on. Unless you are completely sure that there is nobody in there!
- Get your belongings ready for bed before you go out in the evening, or before lights go out in the dorm (this can be early so be prepared)
- Be aware that you will probably have to get out of bed in the dark in the morning and get dressed in the bathroom, get your stuff ready in advance so you can grab it easily
- Don't use a loud alarm in the morning, if you need an alarm then set it to vibrate.

Sleeping

A solid nights sleep can be hard in an Albergue. Our top tips for a good nights sleep are:

- Have ear plugs and an eye mask to block out noise and light
- Listen to a podcast if you can't sleep or the noise of the room is too much

- Wear layers and have layers of bedding to hand to adjust to any temperature, as you won't be able to control the temperature in the dorm room
- Try to keep bags and belongings off the bed if you can – this will give you maximum space but also avoids you making noise in the night and disturbing others
- Don't go to sleep too early if you know you'll wake in the night! There is nothing worse than staring at the ceiling at 0200 counting down the hours until you have to get up and start walking!

Checking out

Be aware that check out tends to be early – 0830 is normal "kick out" time. Normally you'll be out earlier than this, but make sure you've factored this into your plan. Check you've not left anything in your bunk bed or anything plugged in and be on your way!

Seven Habits to Avoid on The Camino

We've touched on this a little already with regard to etiquette in Albergues, but it's worth noting that there are a number of habits that you should try to avoid, where possible, when you are completing your Camino. All of these are based on real life experiences of actual things we've observed on the Camino.

Locomotive Snoring

Most Albergue rooms with be filled with the sounds of gentle snoring all through the night. After a massive walk and a few beers we are all capable of the odd snore. But occasionally, you'll encounter a snorer so dastardly that they will keep the entire room awake ALL NIGHT. This snoring penetrates though ear buds, pillows, even the sound of a lorry speeding down the road wouldn't drown out this person! The worst is the uneven rhythm, the ones who briefly stop snoring just long enough to make you think its stopped, before it suddenly reaches an even more decadent crescendo. AGGHH! I'm not saying snorers shouldn't walk the Camino, we totally expect snoring in a dorm, but if you know you have a serious issue, maybe there are ways to avoid depriving an entire room of any sleep.

Serial Philandering

Lets face it, many people walk the Camino to meet someone and form romantic connections. Totally cool. But don't be the person who has a new fling in every Albergue. Look out for lines like "You're the first girl / boy I've found a connection with on the Camino." Whatever!

You meet a wonderful girl/guy, you fall for the charm and the instant connection, perhaps they woo you. You can't wait to walk the rest of the

Camino with them, maybe stay in touch after the walk. But, they have other ideas. Next day, they're out of here never to be seen again. Soon you'll meet another girl/guy who has also fallen for their lines. You have a serial philanderer on your hands! Run!

Donativo Penny Pinching

The Camino is here for all. It is particularly open to Pilgrims on different budgets. This is why Donativos exist. As mentioned, they are sadly a dying breed of Albergue. It's simple, you donate what you can and what you think that the hospitality is worth. If you cant afford it, that's totally fine. But the absolute worst, are the people who spend loads of cash in bars, or on Camino tat but refuse to pay a fair amount for the Donativo Albergue. Oh, they'll enjoy the 3 course dinner with wine, the roof over their head and the hot water shower in the morning. But they won't donate anything to the people who have worked hard to provide it. Avoid!

Being Gross

Let's face it, nobody is on tip top hygienic form during the Camino. But, there is a spectrum. There's wearing the same socks two days in a row (totally acceptable in my view) then there is totally gross. I'm talking, popping blisters on a bunk bed, bringing walking shoes into the dorm, microwaving your dirty socks, peeing in the shower, barefoot in the toilet, blister plasters dropped on the floor and dirty under-crackers strewn over the bunk beds. C'mon guys don't do it!

Being glued to your phone

Yes. We all want to get to Wi-Fi when we get to our Albergue for the evening. Check on Insta and catch up with friends at home. But it goes a bit far when people are in communal areas face-timing on repeat with ear phones in all night. Maybe they are shy (totally fine) but quite often they are just glued to something else and totally missing their surroundings and the connections they could be making. Let's put down the phones!

Being inconsiderate

We all know that there is an unspoken Albergue rule book. It's quite simple. It has only one rule. When lights are out in the dorm BE QUIET and DO NOT under any circumstances TURN ON THE LIGHTS. If this means you need to get your clothes ready before lights out or get ready in the corridor in the morning, then do it. If someone wakes up your entire room by turning on the light, perhaps with a rousing "Good Morning" to accompany it, make sure you boo and hiss to discourage them.

Becoming a closed group

Its lovely to find new friends and travel on the Camino in groups. But its absolutely rubbish if this means they're shut off to making new connections. What a shame! Its total "you cant sit with us" Mean Girl vibes. Booo to the closed groups

CHAPTER NINE: SOCIALISING AND DOWNTIME

Socialising on the Camino

As part of my research for this book, I was investigating trends related to walking the Camino. One of the trends that I read about was really alarming. Increasingly, Pilgrims walking the Camino are becoming less social, choosing to spend their evenings on their smart phones rather than talking to others. I am an introvert, so I cannot criticise anyone for needing down time, but it seems a real shame to walk the Camino and not spend at least some time socialising. But, I also know that sometimes, the idea of socialising with strangers can be really daunting.

If you need a little helping hand, here's a list of good ice breakers and conversation topics to help get the chat flowing in the evening:

Intro chat:

- Where are you from?
- Where did you walk from today?
- What did you enjoy about your day?
- Where are you going tomorrow?
- Is this your first Camino?
- What job do you do at home?

Getting deeper:

- What was your motivation for walking the Camino?
- What have you found hard about walking?
- What do you think about when you walk?
- How do you think you'll feel when you get to the end?
- Do you think you'll walk the Camino again?
- Have you met any interesting people along the way?

Or, if you'd prefer to keep things light and away from the Camino, how about:

- Do you have any pets?
- What kind of music do you like?
- What's your idea of a perfect day?
- Which celebrity do you most admire?
- What Podcasts/ TV/ movies / books do you like?

Or simply, can I make you a cup of tea/ coffee/ buy you a beer?

Games

If you want to do something a bit more interactive, here's a list of games that you could play in your Albergue in the evening. These can easily be adapted to include people from different backgrounds or people speaking different languages.

One: Two Truths and a Lie

This is a really simple game and a great way to get to know people. The simple premise is that each person (and many people can play it at once) makes two statements that are true and one that is a lie, without revealing which is which. The rest of the group must then guess which one is a lie and explain why. You can be as open or as revealing as you like with the statements you choose.

Two: Who am I?

All you need for this game, are a couple of post it notes or bits of paper and a pen, and a group of people. Taking turns, you write down the name of a famous person and stick it to the forehead of the person next to you, without them seeing the name. Each person is then allowed to ask one question to try to identify who they are, but these must be "yes" or "no" questions. For example, "Am I an actress?" The winner is the first person to guess who they are. Remember if you play this with an international crowd, to make sure that the famous people are widely known.

Three: Categories

In this game, somebody chooses a category, for example "Airlines" or "Cocktails" and you all take it in turn to name something from that category. This can be really fun with an international group as you might learn new things.

Alternatively, if you have a pack of cards, with you, then there are lots of games you could play that most people would be able to join in with!

Down Time and Reflection

As mentioned in previous chapters, the Camino offers such a fantastic opportunity to spend some time thinking and contemplating. I use a journaling practise to help put some order to my thoughts. I found this really valuable when walking the Camino. Even if you don't do this, at the very least, I'd recommend keeping a short diary to record your experience. It takes 5 minutes each day and it is something that you can come back to in future. Yes, photos are fantastic memories, but you'll quickly forget all the amazing experiences you've had along the way if you don't write them down.

Diary

- Distance walked
- From where to where

- Where I stayed overnight
- What the route was like
- Who I met today

Journaling

In addition to keeping a diary, if you want to use a journaling practise during your Camino, here's what I would recommend.

- What did I find challenging today?
- What did I enjoy today?
- Record any uncomfortable thoughts that came up during the day
- Record any positive thoughts that came up during the day
- What do I want to do more of or find more of tomorrow?

These are just ideas and I'd suggest making the journal questions relevant to you and your experience.

CHAPTER TEN: THE WALKING

Choosing who to walk with?

Choosing who to walk the Camino with is another big decision that you should make before you start. Or to at least consider whether you want to walk all of it, some of it, or none of it alone.

The next section will provide some points to consider when deciding whether to walk the Camino solo, in a group or as a couple. I will also highlight some tips that can help to make walking the Camino go as smoothly as possible, depending on the choice that you make.

Walking the Camino Solo

Walking the Camino solo can be a great option. If you are looking for an empowering experience and plenty of time to think, then being solo can be of benefit. But let's break it down a little further.

Firstly, you are never truly alone on the Camino. Unless you choose to walk an unusual route, in the height of winter, you aren't "alone". You will see so many pilgrims on the walk itself, as well as at lunch spots and in the Albergues in the evening. Even if you choose to walk alone during the day, you will have the option to socialise in the evening or just to break the silence with small talk over lunch. Of course, you can choose to be completely alone if that's what you are looking for.

Secondly, you will always have the choice to change your mind about walking solo and find a friend to walk with, if you want to. Or walk a couple of days on your own and a couple with others. Plenty of people I met, spent the days walking alone and re-joined the same group each night.

Finally, if you choose to join the Camino solo, but intend to find others to walk with from the outset, this will be very easy. It's completely normal to strike up a conversation with others on the Camino and ask if you can walk together. You're sure to find others in the same position who are keen to hang out.

Walking the Camino as a couple

We walked the Camino as a couple, so we have quite a bit of insight into this experience.

Firstly, I think we would both agree that this was one of the best experiences we've ever had as a couple. Other couples I have met have shared this sentiment too. Whilst walking the Camino, you're bound to see a new side to each other, as well as having the opportunity to spend some quality time together. For us, we found that our bond grew stronger from the intimacy of going through this experience together. We learnt to trust each other more, the importance of teamwork and how to help each other through challenging times. We also had a lot of fun and laughter.

If you choose to walk the Camino as a couple, we have a few tips for you below.

#1 Agree what you both hope to achieve from walking the Camino as a couple

Walking the Camino de Santiago is a life-affirming experience for some. For others, it might just be a physical challenge or a bit of fun. We all have a personal reason for choosing to walk the Camino de Santiago.

When you walk together as a couple, it's important to understand each other's individual motivation as well as knowing what you both want to achieve together. Knowing this, means that you can check in with each other to ensure you're getting what you need and want.

#2 Discuss acomodation options

On the Camino de Santiago there are multiple accommodation options. Some legs of the journey have both Municipal Albergues, and Private Albergues. Municipal tend to be more basic than the private, but both options are essentially a bunk bed in a dormitory and shared space. Then there are Pensions, which have private rooms and are mostly still fairly basic. All the way up to, private hotels.

For couples, staying only in dormitories for a month can be a challenge. For me, personal space was important, so we agreed in advance to stay in dorm rooms about 70% of the time and private rooms for 30%. But at various points throughout the month, this balance changed. But every day, we discussed it and made sure we were both happy with the choice.

#3 Set a budget

This is important for anyone walking the Camino de Santiago. You want to be able to enjoy each day without stressing that you are spending too much money. As a couple, even more so.
Check in advance that you have a similar idea of how much money you are willing to spend. But also, how you want to spend that money. Is it more important to eat out every day? Or spend money on better accommodation?

#4 Understand how much you both want to socialise

Particularly if one of you is more introverted than the other, it can be a good idea to set expectations. Consider whether you want to walk with other

Pilgrims during the day or just socialise in the evening? Do you want to go with the flow? Or do you own thing? One of you might one to read in the evening, whilst the other spends all night chatting to others.

#5 Understand that your experience might be different to solo walkers

Walking together is really special. But there might be times when you feel a pang of jealously that you perhaps aren't as free to take your own path, as solo travellers. That said, you also have a companion with you every step of the way acting as your number one cheerleader.

#6 Find a walking pace to suit you both

This one is pretty important! Make sure you both have a rough idea of how much ground you want to cover each day – if one of you is used to walking 30km a day and other has never walked more than 5km, then you need to find a middle ground. If one partner is taller, or fitter, then the pace you naturally walk will be different.

To avoid injury, frustration or arguments, consider how you'll manage one of you walking quicker than the other. Will the faster walker drop back to the slower pace? Or if somebody is less fit, do they need to put in more training before you go?

#7 Or, consider walking separately sometimes
This might sound dramatic, but you could

consider walking separately some of the time. This might be particularly helpful if one of you is much quicker than the other. We walk at a similar pace, so tended to stick together, but I met other couples who sometimes walked a few hours separately and met up for lunch.

#8 Give each other time to reflect

All couples may not need this, but it's something that we found really positive. We gave each other a little time during the day to listen to a Podcast, or audio book. We also found time separately in the evening to reflect on our days in our own ways – writing a journal for me!

#9 Understand your argument trigger points

Ooof, this is big! When you're walking the Camino, sometimes (often) you will be hungry and tired! We had some almighty arguments, mostly driven by me being HANGRY. Once I'd realised this was the cause, things got better.

You might be one of those couples who argues very little, but I feel like even the most sedate pairs will argue at least once during the Camino.

#10 Embrace the adventure and have fun

Being together and walking 24 7? Utter madness. But also, utterly fun! And it may not be something you ever get to do again. Embrace it!

Walking in a group

Are you thinking about walking the Camino with a big group of friends? Awesome. You'll have an amazing experience. A bit like walking as a couple, this is a great way to get to know your friends better and to have fun together.

There are a few considerations you should also take into account in your group.

#1 Walking Pace

Within a group, you're likely to all walk at different paces naturally. Of course, it's possible you have similar fitness levels and heights and therefore walk the same pace, but if this is not the case then you may need to consider how best to manage the differences.

A good option can be to walk at the slowest person's pace, this avoids injury. But it could be frustrating if the slowest person is significantly different to others. Alternatively, if you're a big group, you may be able to split into smaller groups with similar paces.

Groups I've met on the Camino have chosen to walk apart for a few hours at a time, then meet back up later in the evening.

#2 Alone time

The Camino can be quite intense, there may be

times when one or more of the group need some alone time. Of course, if you're good friends already then you will be aware of how much alone time each other needs. But, it can be good to make sure everyone has enough down time to avoid tempers becoming frayed.

#3 Accommodation choices

On many of the Camino stages, there are some options for acomodation. For example, you may have the choice between municipal and private Albergues. The municipal tends to be cheaper, but very basic. If you're in a large group, it can be useful to set expectations in advance. Many people will hate how primitive the municipal Albergues are, and others will be OK with it. In a group, you may need to compromise.

The other thing to be aware of as a group is that you may not always be able to get space in the same Albergue. Unless you arrive early or book in advance, there may be times, especially in a large group when you will not be able to stay altogether.

#4 Meeting other people

The final point to make about walking the Camino as a group, is that you should try to avoid being totally closed off to new people. A big part of the appeal of walking the Camino, is the interesting and varied people you'll meet. If you walk the Camino with friends from home, it can be easy to stay in this little bubble and not let anybody else in.

Motivation During the Walk

What do to whilst you are walking

Many people choose to walk each day on the Camino alone and often in silence. They find that this gives them lots of time to think and focus only on the steps that they are taking. Others find that they need a little more interaction and entertainment.

When we walked the Camino, we both enjoyed listening to Podcasts, music and audio books at different points in the day. Partly this was because we were both so tired in the morning, that it was best not to talk! Instead, we would plug in our earphones for the first two hours and actively ignore each other. Sometimes this is better than behaving like bears with sore heads.

One thing I found whilst walking and listening to podcasts and audio books, is that I could really absorb the information I was listening to. Often, particularly during the pandemic, I found I couldn't focus on anything, let alone listen to a story. But, when it's just you and the open road and some sound in your ears, it's so much easier to focus.

From listening to podcasts and audio books, I discovered some amazing new information and also had time for self-reflection. Someone I met on my first Camino had been walking in silence previously but decided to listen to an audio book after I suggested it to her. She said that this was the best day of walking! It may seem that it's not "purist" to have headphones in, but I found that it actually enabled me to focus more on the walking and fall into a meditative state, than if I'd been walking in silence.

In my view, if you've got time to fill, why not use it to listen to some new music or learn something? The one caution, is to make sure you don't block out everything around you by putting headphones in. Wearing headphones can be an indicator to others that you don't want to walk with them or socialise. If that's the case, then great! But if you do want to chat to others, maybe keep the headphone wearing down to just a few hours.

Our favourite podcasts to listen to were *The Rest is History* (a fun way to learn), *Desert Island Discs* (music and intimate celeb interviews with an extensive back catalogue) and *Off Menu* (if you like food and comedy, this ones a good one for you.)

Whatever you choose, you'll get into your own rhythm after a few days and it will start to feel like a nice routine and the miles will fly by.

Sectioning your day

Some days walking the Camino can be long. Of

course, looking back, we enjoyed every moment. But at the time, with 30 km in front of you, motivation can sometimes feel like a challenge. One way that we overcame this feeling, was to section up our day.

First Coffee

On every Camino we've walked, the first coffee of the day has always been our first target. Oftentimes we left so early in the morning that it was difficult to face breakfast or a coffee in the Albergue. We also didn't really want to hang around too long, especially in the summer when the weather heats up quickly in the morning.

Instead, we would find a target on the map, usually around 10km away and aim for this to be our first break. The Café Con Leche (CCL) for my partner and Café Solo (CS) for me became rather a ritual, and we would chant CCL or CS at each other as we walked in the morning.

Not only did this give us a motivational goal, but it was a particularly great feeling to know that we've hit 10km before stopping. A psychological boost! Others I've met on the Camino do something slightly similar, but perhaps with different distance targets. For example, the 10 miles before 10:00 can be a good target, especially if it's a very hot day.

Lunch Time

It's important on the Camino to maintain your calorie intake and stop for a good lunch. On longer days, we tried to limit lunch breaks to 30 minutes, sometimes even 15. But some of the most memorable lunch breaks we had were around an hour long. There's something about stopping to smell the roses, that makes it all worthwhile.

If you do stop for a while, make sure you stretch a little to stop your body from seizing up and replace any layers. You can cool down quite quickly after sweating a lot when you walk.

Along the way, if you do one of the main routes, there are normally plenty of places to stop for lunch. That said, on the North Route, there are some stretches with very little. One day, we had to settle for a coin operated vending machine – suffice to say, our change only stretched as far as a packet of stale biscuits.

It can be sensible to check the route for the next day, the day before you set out. If there are long sections without any cafes or restaurants, check if there are supermarkets. If there are no food shops, then consider packing a lunch and taking it with you.

More often than not, we packed a lunch with us. We found this was the cheapest option, but also gave us total flexibility on when we could stop. We discovered some epic lunch spots perched atop a cliff, by rivers or just overlooking stunning vistas.

Well worth the pre-planning and it's pretty easy to pop a baguette into your backpack!

Power Drink

It can be risky to indulge in an alcoholic drink during the day when you're walking. Especially if the weather is hot. Besides, sometimes it's better to wait to the evening and enjoy it properly.
But, if you do need a little boost in the afternoon, I'll give you this cheeky tip!

If you're struggling with less than about 7km to go, a small cold beverage can do wonders for the spirits. We called it "Power Hour", the little spring in your step that can only be achieved by enjoying a small sangria or beer.

Other breaks

As well as the above, we tried to take small breaks at fairly regular intervals throughout the day. We found it best to target and plan when these were to give us a bit of focus. Unplanned stops can start to feel a bit wearing after some time. If you have any foot pain, a small break and a chance to take off your shoes can do wonders.

It probably sounds incredibly basic, but we would highly recommend scheduling toilet breaks on the Camino. There are times when you won't see a café for miles and the nature toilet is your only option. But if a nature toilet won't quite cut it, then it can be good to have a plan for where you'll stop to use the bathroom (if you catch my drift!)

Being in the moment

Just a final note on walking. It can be really easy to get bogged down with targets and how far you have to walk each day. Particularly if you're in pain, or struggling in the heat, your mind can easily get into a negative thought pattern.

If you spend the entire walk rushing through, focused on getting through each day, you'll miss a lot of the benefits. Where you can, do try to stay "in the moment" and enjoy the walk. We feel so lucky to have walked more than one Camino, but for many people, it's a once in a lifetime experience. So don't let it flash by you.

My tip for staying present if you find that you're in a negative thought pattern, is to stop, sit down and take a few deep breaths. Just taking a second to appreciate what's around you will really help you to gain perspective.

CHAPTER ELEVEN: STAYING HEALTHY ON THE ROAD

If this is the first time that you've lived out of a backpack, and the first time that you've walked long distances every day, then it's likely that you might find it difficult to maintain your health and fitness whilst walking the Camino. Whilst we are not medical or fitness experts, we've collated some top tips through research, our own experience and the experience of our fellow Pilgrims.

Nutrition

Calorie Intake

It's really difficult to confidently say how many extra calories that you burn, and therefore need to consume, whilst walking the Camino. This varies according to your height and weight and normal metabolic functioning.

I walked about 30km per day and on average, found that I was burning an additional 1,500 to 2,000 calories per day. This means that my overall calorie deficit per day was between 3,500 and 4,000 per day. I found that no matter how much I ate, I was constantly hungry. It's actually quite difficult to consume 4,000 good calories per day.

If you're keen to dine out, try the Menu Del Dia's which you can find in most Spanish restaurants. They range between 10 and 20 Euros and include three courses, bread and a drink. Just what every Pilgrim needs to keep up their calories!

There are also times on the Camino when you won't find a supermarket or a cafe for a long distance. I would suggest always packing an emergency snack, just in case this happens. Dried fruit and nuts can be excellent, as they won't melt or go off in your bag and provide excellent protein and calories.

Maintaining Fruit and Veg Intake

Especially if you don't have regular access to a kitchen, it can be tricky to maintain your normal levels of fruit and veg intake. Of course, if you do have a kitchen, and you have time to cook then you could easily whip up a salad or some vegetable pasta in the evening.

To keep your fruit and veg intake up during the day, these are our Lotus Eaters Travel, top tips:

- Carton of gazpacho – you can buy this in most supermarkets, it's cold tomato soup that also has garlic and onion. It makes an excellent lunch (with bread) or a snack to enjoy throughout the day.
- Fresh tomatoes and cucumber in your sandwiches or with bread – tomatoes and cucumber are cheap, fresh and readily available in Spain and Portugal
- Snack on fruit – bananas or peaches work well to put in your backpack
- Order Tostada con Tomate (toast topped with fresh tomatoes) available in most Spanish cafes
- If you're ordering from the Menu Del Dia, often there will be a salad available as a starter, or a soup.

If you're not confident that you will be able to maintain your normal levels of vitamin intake, why not pack a multi-vitamin tablet with you. You could decant the correct number of tablets into a ziplock bag so that you don't need to carry the entire pack.

Water Consumption

NHS guidelines (National Health Service in the UK) suggest that everyone should drink between 6 to 8 glasses of water (approx 1.2 to 1.5 litres) per day as a minimum.[xi]

Of course, this increases when you're exercising or sweating through excessive heat. Therefore, when walking, especially in the summer, it's important to drink more than you normally would. Take regular water breaks, or even better if you've got access to water easily as you walk. Good practise is to fill up your water bottle every time you see a water fountain or every time you stop for coffee, fill it up in the cafe. I would also take a bottle to bed with me as the Albergues can be hot through the night and you might need to replenish fluids.

Preventing Injury

One of the most important things you can do to prevent injury whilst walking the Camino, is to prioritise your sleep. This can be really challenging, especially in noisy Albergues, but try to make sure that you get enough sleep for your body to re cooperate. It is during sleep that your body is able to mend itself.

The other key thing you can do is look after your legs and feet, which will be taking a daily battering.

Here are the Lotus Eaters Travel Top Tips:

- Bathe your feet daily in warm or cool water and massage them whilst rubbing in some moisturiser. The moisturiser will help to prevent blisters as it reduces friction in your shoes when you walk.
- Elevate your legs. Your legs suffer so much punishment when walking the Camino, they are the most impacted parts of your

body. At the end of each walking day, after or before your shower, lay against the wall with your legs up in the air resting. You can do this on a top or bottom bunk bed easily too. Even just a few minutes will help to release the pressure on your legs. If you are really struggling with muscular pain in your legs or feet, then prop your feet up on a blanket through the night when you sleep. A physio I met on my first Camino gave me this tip and I haven't looked back.

- If you normally use a foam roller to help relieve muscle pain or prevent injury, you can buy travel size foam rollers to take on the way with you. Or, my cheap alternative, is to use a tennis ball. I used this every day when walking my first Camino to release the tension in my thigh and glute muscles.
- If you think you might need knee or ankle supports, then pack them with you. Better to have them and not use them, that need support and wait days to find a pharmacy to find it.
- Finally, stretch! A stretch in the morning and evening, even just a few minutes, will work wonders for your flexibility and muscle performance throughout the day.

For back and shoulder health, the best thing you

can possibly do is keep your backpack as light as possible!

Common Ailments on the Camino

There are a few issues to look out for whilst walking the Camino.

1) Sun stroke and sun burn
2) Disney Rash (similar to heat rash) and other chafing issues
3) The hangover
4) Dehydration
5) Mosquito and insect bites
6) Blisters and infected blisters.

We are not medical experts, but if you know the signs of these ailments and how to prevent them, then you can help yourself and your Camino friends. We hear that number three is particularly savage.

CHAPTER TWELVE: CAMINO DE SANTIAGO DAILY STAGES

When it comes to creating your itinerary, we would highly recommend the Buen Camino App. This intuitive app (which is free to download), helps you to craft a personalised plan for your individual route, tailoring according to the distance you plan to walk and alerting you to the amenities in each stopping place. You may be someone who likes to plan in advance, or equally somebody who would prefer to adapt their plan each day "the go with the flow" approach. Either way, Buen Camino is a very useful tool.

To help you prepare, we have also set out some suggested itineraries for the three major routes – North Route, French Route and Portuguese Route from Porto. These itineraries are based on walking in the range of 20 to 30km each day, but this may not suit your requirements. We have also tailored these itineraries to incorporate some of the "must see" places, which are our own Lotus Eaters Travel recommendations.

The North Route (Norte)

The natural starting point of the Camino North Route is Irun. This is a small and "typical" Spanish town, just across the border from France. The nearest airport is actually Biarritz, where you can take a short train to Hendaye, cross the border (notional border, there is no checkpoint) and then reach Irun on a second short train.

You can collect your Credential from the main Pilgrim Albergue in Irun. In Irun, you have the option to spend your first night in the Municipal Albergue. If you're really keen to start with other Pilgrims and meet as many other people as possible, then this is a good idea. But we've heard that it is one of the worst Albergue's on the Camino North Route. So, firstly, if you do stay here, don't be alarmed if it feels a bit like a prison (it does), the rest of the Albergues on the route are mainly not like this. Secondly, if you choose not to stay there, then don't worry, you will have plenty of chances to meet people

Day 1: Irun to San Sebastian 26km

Day 2: San Sebastian to Zarautz 21km

Day 3: Zarautz to Barrio de Ibiri 27km

Day 4: Barrio de Ibri to Zenarruza 26km

Day 5: Zenarruza to Gernika 18km

Day 6: Gerninka to Bilbao 32km

Day 7: Bilbao to Pobena 26km

Day 8: Pobena to Castro Uridales 30km (Taking in some Tapas in Castro Uridales is a **Lotus Eaters Travel Must See**)

Day 9: Castro Uridales to Laredo 30km(Staying at the Convent (Albergue Casa de la Trinidad) in Laredo is a **Lotus Eaters Travel Must See**. Enjoy the sociable communal dinner and the hospitality offered by the fantastic Nuns in this beautiful building.)

Day 10: Laredo to Guemes 30km (Guemes, one of the oldest Albergue's on the North Route is undoubtedly a **Lotus Eaters Travel Must See**. The owner of this Donativo Albergue will entertain you for hours, the facilities are wonderful and the communal dinner is a convivial experience.)

Day 11: Guemes to Santander 10km (with a boat ride from Somo to Santander). Many people choose to continue further on this day, but we chose to take in Santander.

Day 12: Santander to Santillana del Mar 37km (This is a long day, but worth it to enjoy the night in Santander. Also, note advice below about skipping some of the walks out of the major cities. There is an option to do that today).

Day 13: Santialla del Mar to Comillas 22km

Day 14: Comillas to Colombres 29km

Day 15: Colombres to Llanes 23km

Day 16: Llanes to San Esteban de Lecces 34km

Day 17: San Esteban de Lecces to Villavicisosa 33km

Day 18: Villavicisosa to Gijon 29km

Day 19: Gijon to Aviles 25km

Day 20: Aviles to Soto de Luna 36km

Day 21: Soto de Luna to Luarca 34km

Day 22: Luarca to Navia 20km

Day 23: Navia to Tapia de Casariego 21km (a detour onto the coastal variant route to stay in the stunning Tapia de Casareigo).

Day 24: Casareigo to Ribadeo 11km (take time to stop at the beach in Playa de Penarronda, which is a **Lotus Eaters Travel Must See**)

Day 25: Ribadeo to Lourenza 27km

Day 26: Lourenza to As Parades (Castromaior) 22km (the mountain route to Abadin is a **Lotus Eaters Travel Must See.** It is steep and there are no facilities up there so pack lunch, but it is stunning). We also recommend passing Abadin and staying in As Parades in the stunning Albergue O Xistral.

Day 27: As Parades to Baamonde 33km

Day 28: Baamonde to Sobrado dos Monxes 32km (this is a shorter route, you will be given the option but we recommend taking the shorter route as it is beautiful).

Day 29: Sobrado dos Monxes to Salceda 34km

Day 30: Salceda to Santiago 27km (book in advance and try to get the Albergue with the pool in A Salceda)

On the North Route, we have five main pieces of advice when you craft your itinerary:

One: You'll notice there are numerous opportunities to take a "blue" route as an alternative coastal path, rather than a yellow route. Where possible, take the blue routes. They will not disappoint. Some of them can be tough to walk, with steep hills and narrow paths, but they offer unparalleled sea views.

Two: There are some accommodation gaps where Albergue's have closed during the pandemic and not re-opened. Look out for these when you plan your day as you may need to walk further than expected, or arrive early to town to secure

your space in an Albergue.

Three: It can be tempting, especially if you're on a budget, to skip the big cities like San Sebastian, Bilbao and Santander. You can stay in and enjoy these cities on a budget if you want to. Please don't miss them as they are such an amazing part of the North Route. If there is no space in Albergues, perhaps you could find another Pilgrim and book a private room and split the cost.

Four: Try to build in enough time to enjoy the beaches, especially in the summer. A swim at the end of a hard day of walking is such an incredible feeling! The North Coast also offers fantastic surfing, if you want to give that a go.

Five: Some of the Camino, into and out of, the major cities are not the best routes. The path runs through heavy industrial areas and frankly, it's really boring! We chose to avoid some of this trudgery and occasionally took metros or trains to avoid it – for some people, this will feel like "cheating", but if you'd rather save your legs and your time, then go for it. For example, into Bilbao, you can get a train from Lezama and then start again from Portugalte rather than walking out of the city.

The French Route (Frances)

The French Route is the busiest and most popular of the longer Camino Routes. It was perhaps made even more famous by the movie "The Way", which depicts the French route. Subsequently, it has far more infrastructure than the North Route, which enables you to walk on average shorter distances each day. The recommended itinerary below takes 32 days, despite covering a shorter distance than the North Route covers in 30 days. However, if you wanted to, you could truncate a few days on the French route to finish the route in a shorter time period. The flexibility of the French route is one of the advantages.

The official starting point of the French route, according to the Pilgrims Office of Santiago, is Roncesvalles therefore many Spanish people start at this point. Others choose to start a day earlier in St-Jean Pied de Port, but be aware that the walk from here to Roncesvalles is a tough one! If you choose to start in Roncesvalles, then book accommodation in advance as it gets busy, especially in peak season.

Day 1: Saint-Jean-Pied-de-Port to Roncesvalles 24.7km

Day 2: Roncesvalles to Zubiri 22.3km

Day 3: Zubiri to Pamplona 21.1km (Pamplona is a **Lotus Eaters Travel Must See**, even when the bulls aren't running Pamplona is a delightful city and well worth spending a night).

Day 4: Pamplona to Puente la Reina 23.7km

Day 5: Puente la Reina to Estella 21.9km

Day 6: Estella to Los Arcos 21.4km (Don't miss out on seeing, and drinking from, the wine fountain at Bodega Irache today, a **Lotus Eaters Travel Must See**).

Day 7: Los Arcos to Logroño 27.7km (Logrono is a **Lotus Eaters Travel Must See**, do not miss out on a glass of Rioja in this, the capital of the Rioja region.)

Day 8: Logroño to Nájera 28.3km

Day 9: Nájera to Santo Domingo de la Calzada 20.9km

Day 10: Santo Domingo to Belorado 22.7km

Day 11: Belorado to San Juan de Ortega 23.9km

Day 12: San Juan de Ortega to Burgos 26km

Day 13: Burgos to Hornillos del Camino 20.9km

Day 14: Hornillos del Camino Castrojeriz 19.9km

Day 15: Castrojeriz to Frómista 25.2km

Day 16: Frómista to Carrión de los Condes 18.9km

Day 17: Carrión de los Condes to Ledigos 23.2km

Day 18: Ledigos to Sahagún 15.2km

Day 19: Sahagún to Bercianos del Real Camino 25.9km

Day 20: Bercianos del Real Camino to Mansilla de las Mulas 26.2km

Day 21: Mansilla de las Mulas to León 24.6km

Day 22: León to San Martín del Camino 23.7km

Day 23: San Martín del Camino to Astorga 23.7km

Day 24: Astroga to Foncebadón 25.8km

Day 25: Foncebadón to Ponferrada 26.8km

Day 26: Ponferrada to Villafranca del Bierzo 24.2km

Day 27: Villafranca del Bierzo to O Cebreiro 28.8km

Day 28: O Cebreiro to Triacastela 20.9km

Day 29: Triacastela to Sarria 24.2km

Day 30: Sarria to Portomarín 22km (Don't forget to start collecting two stamps per day at this stage, if you want to collect your Compostela in Santiago).

Day 31: Portomarín to Palas de Rei 25.4km

Day 32: Padas de Rei to Arzúa 28.5km

Day 33: Arzúa to Pedrouzo 19.5km

Day 34: Pedrouo to Santiago de Compostela 19.9km

The Portuguese Route

We highly recommend starting off in Porto. Some people do walk from Lisbon to Porto, but we've heard and read that it is not a very beautiful walk, you will not meet many people and the Albergues are not as good as on the Porto to Santiago stretch.

In any event, Porto is an amazing city and a fantastic place to kick off your Camino adventures. if you can, spend some time in Porto enjoying the sights and sounds. At least 24 hours, but if you can take two days to enjoy it you will not regret it. There is an excellent Albergue in Porto (Albergue de Perigrinos Porto), where we would recommend that you start. Unlike the Albergue in Irun (at the start of the Norte) it's a really nice place to stay, with hammocks in the garden. You can purchase your Credential from this Albergue, or from the Cathedral in the centre of Porto.

As you leave Porto and start on your Camino, we strongly recommend spending the first couple of days on the Senda Litoral Route (not the Coastal route, but the route that hugs the coast – yes, quite confusing!) The central route out of Porto mainly navigates industrial areas, hence it's much more scenic to spend a few days on the coast instead. We would then recommend rejoining the inland route, if you're looking for a good insight into Portuguese countryside life. The full coastal route tends to be quieter, and it seems a shame to miss some of the inland Portuguese scenery. But you could opt to take the full coastal route and rejoin the inland route around Redondela if you wanted to extend your time on the coast. Much of this decision might be dictated by the weather, if the weather is inclement then we would recommend heading inland which is much warmer and more sheltered. If you have good weather, and want to make the most of it, and enjoy the coastal breeze, then stick with the coast or the Senda Litoral.

Day 1: Porto to Labruge 19km (Walking along the board walks out of Porto is a **Lotus Eaters Travel Must See**).

Day 2: Labruge to Sao Pedro De Rates 21km (via Vila Do Conde where you should stop for lunch) (this rejoins the central route now.)

Day 3: Sao Pedro De Rates to Barcelos 16km

Day 4: Barcelos to Ponte De Lima 34km (this is a long day, but Ponte De Lima is a **Lotus Eaters Travel Must See**).

Day 5: Ponte de Lima to Rubiaes 18km

Day 6: Rubiaes to Valenca 17.5km (you could cross into Tui today or stay in Valenca to enjoy one last night in Portugal) (Valenca Fort is a **Lotus Eaters Travel Must See**).

Day 7: Valenca to A Rua (Mos) 28km (Take the alternative trail at Orbenlle, this will make a longer day but is much more pleasant.)

Day 8: A Rua (Mos) to Pontevedra 30km (If you wanted to take a rest day at this point, Pontevedra is a bustling tourist town with lots to see and some fantastic restaurants).

Day 9: Pontevedra to Caldas de Reis 21km

Day 10: Caldas de Reis to Vilar 24km (Many people choose to stay in Padron on their last night before Santiago. If your budget can stretch, we recommend passing Padron to stay in O Lagar De Jesus Albergue in Vilar. It is absolutely stunning and a **Lotus Eaters Travel Must See**. It is slightly more expensive than a Municipal Albergue but in our view worth the money.)

Day 11: Vilar to Santiago 19km

If you wanted to, you could also slow down this itinerary and spend longer in Portugal.

If you choose not to take the coastal route out of Porto (which in our view, would be a big shame), then stop by the Monastery of Vairao (around 25km North of Porto), which is really popular with those walking the central route.

The central route does get quite busy and most people walk similar itineraries from town to town. If you're not a fan of staying in towns and you'd rather avoid the crowds, then a good tip can be to stay in more remote Albergue's before or after the major towns on route. This means that you will be walking out of step with the main crowds and can have a bit more of a chance for escapism. But make sure you check whether the Albergue's serve food if there are no restaurants or shops nearby.

The other experience worth an honourable mention, is the opportunity to canoe up the river to Tui. You can take a canoe trip from Caminha to Tui, or vice versa depending on your starting point. We haven't tried this but have met a group of people who raved about it. I can't quite decide if this feels like "cheating" to row rather than walk part of the Camino, but either way, it sounds like a hell of an experience.

CHAPTER THIRTEEN: THE LAST 100KM AND THE CAMINO FINISTERRE

The next chapter will provide detailed itineraries for the last 100km of the three most popular Camino routes. Many people each year choose to walk just the last 100km into Santiago, chiefly because this is the minimum distance, you're required to cover on foot to be awarded with a Compostela certificate in Compostela. However, even if you are intending to walk a full Camino route, putting a little extra planning into the last 100km can be very helpful, as these sections of the trail tend to get busy in peak season.

The last 100km of the Camino Portuguese Route – From Tui to Santiago

The walk from Tui to Santiago, follows the Camino de Santiago Portuguese Route. In an ideal world, we would recommend walking from Porto to Santiago. The full route from Porto takes in rolling countryside, sweeping coast and the best of Portugal and Spain. But, to walk the 260km (280km on the coast) you need between 10 and 14 full days. Tui to Santiago however is just over 100km and can be walked over 5km at a swift pace.

Five reasons to walk from Tui to Santiago

1// The last 100km of the Portuguese route (from Tui to Santiago) is quieter than the last 100km of the French route, or the North route. In fact, the French and North route merge over the last 100km, so the paths become quite busy. This is especially true in the summer months.

2// You can walk from Tui to Santiago in a short period of time - 5 days is the average. This means, you could take one week off work and still have some time left to enjoy Santiago when you get there.

3// The walk is fairly flat and easy terrain to walk on. This, coupled with the ease of navigation on the Camino, means that this hike will suit newbies or novices. This stretch of the Camino, as with all routes, is very well kitted out for hikers. In particular, we noticed that Pilgrim accommodation is plentiful on this stretch. Plus, there are lots of catering options with regular restaurants, bars and cafes along the way.

4// You can spend a day in Portugal, just across the river from Tui, before you start the Camino. If you're keen to see some of Portugal, this is really easy to do. Simply walk over the bridge (aptly named the friendship bridge) from Tui and you'll be in the charming town of Valenca.

5// As Tui is just over 100km from Santiago, you can get your Compostela (certificate) when you arrive in Santiago if you wish to. Just make sure you get two stamps per day in our credential. Find out more about this here.

Where is Tui?

Tui is a town in the south of Pontevedra in Galicia in Spain. It sits on the river Mino directly across from the Portuguese town of Valenca.

Tui is quite easy to get to making the town an accessible start point to walk part of the Camino. The nearest airport is Vigo which is approximately 12 miles from the start of the Camino in Tui. Check flights to Vigo here on Skyscanner.

The unassuming but beautiful town is known for both it's cathedral and castle. It boasts several great restaurants and bars, as well as accommodation options. Being perched on top of a hill, you can also see the river from the town.

How to walk from Tui to Santiago?

The actual distance to walk from Tui to Santiago is 119km. You can do this over five or six days, depending on your pace. Here are the three main options that most people take when walking from Tui to Santiago:

Five Days (Option One):

Tui to Redondela (31km or 32.5km)
Redondela to Pontevedra (19.5km)
Pontevedra to Caldas de Reis (21km)
Caldas de Reis to Vilar (24.5km)
Vilar to Santiago de Compostela (19km)

Five Days (Option Two):

Tui to A Rua (Mos) (21km)
A Rua (Mos) to Pontevedra (29.5km)
Pontevedra to Caldas de Reis (21km)
Caldas de Reis to Vilar (or Padron) (24.5km or 19km if remaining if staying in Padron)
Vilar to Santiago de Compostela (19km or 25km from Padron)

Six Days:

Tui to O Porriño (16km)
O Porriño to Redondela (15km)
Redondela to Pontevedra (19.5km)
Pontevedra to Caldas de Reis (21km)
Caldas de Reis to Padron (19km)

Padron to Santiago de Compostela (25km)

Below, we've set out in detail the five stages of walking from Tui to Santiago that we took during our walk from Porto to Santiago in 2022. We walked the five-day (option one) route. But we would very much recommend the five day (option two) route for anyone walking **only** from Tui to Santiago (i.e. not walking the entire Porto to Santiago route).

The five stages from Tui to Santiago

Day One: Tui to Redondela

We decided to walk the 31km from Tui to Redondela in one day. If you're taking the six day route, you will stop overnight in O Poriño after around 16km. However, we decided to stay in Redondela as it looked nicer and we were in our stride.

You could also split and stay in A Rua (Mos) which is about 20km from Tui - as set out in Option Two above. I would recommend staying in A Rua (Mos) if you'd prefer not to walk more than 30km. A Rua (Mos) is a very small town with just one bar and one Albergue, but it's very pretty.

Distance: 31km (32.5km if you take the longer route)

Highlights: The trail through the forest at around 5km was a welcome break from the road walking.

Route: On route to O Poriño there is a choice of direction at Orbnelle. You can take the left-hand trail, longer and more scenic, or the right hand one which takes you through and industrial area but is more direct. The industrial route is not pretty and we would highly recommend turning left and taking the slightly longer route.

Food and accommodation: Redondela has nine Albergues! It's a veritable feast. But, be aware this town is the merging point for the Portuguese Coastal and Central routes, plus into the last 100km before Santiago, so it does get busy. We chose Avoa Regina which has great facilities and is bookable on Booking.com at 15 Euros per night. There are quite a few pizza places and tapas bars in the centre of town. If you stay at Avoa Regina do not miss out on breakfast the next morning across the road.

Day Two: Redondela to Pontevedra

Distance: 19.5km

Highlights: A few nice trails take you off the road and a bar (Casa Fermin) 5km short of Potenvedra is great for a coffee or cerveza.

Route: On route, you'll find cafe and food options at Arcade around 8km in, plus a few bars towards the end of the walk. There are a few hills today, both climb to 150m and are over quite swiftly. There are around 6km on trail and the rest or road/

pavement. At O Pobo you have an option to carry on the main route or take a trail through forest. The trail is not much longer and far prettier than the road.

Food and Accommodation: Pontevedra has six Albergues, some Pensions and also hotels. It's a bit of a tourist town for Spanish travellers so prices can get high for private rooms. Lots of restaurants with Menu del Dia plus some higher end places and of course some supermarkets.

Day Three: Pontevedra to Caldas de Reis

Distance: 21km

Highlights: Arrival in Caldas de Reis with its plentiful bars and restaurants

Route: A swift 21km today with only one small hill. Mostly road and navigating quiet areas with limited big towns.

Food and Accommodation: We stayed at Martinez Rooms Pilgrims in a private room. There are many other albergue options. Pilgrim menus are offered at a few restaurants in town.

Day Four: Caldas de Reis to Vilar

We chose to walk past Padron on this day and stay in Vilar because we had a booking at O Lagar de Jesus Albergue (which is one of our favourites on the whole route!) Many people stay in Padron, which has a municipal albergue.

Distance: 24.5km

Highlights: The trails were lovely, pine trees and smattering of sun light coming through.

Route: The route is quite straightforward, but with one small climb (around 200m). There are approximately 3km on trails and the rest on roads, but the trails feel longer than that and the roads are quiet and picturesque. Some industrial areas too.

Food and Accommodation: In Vilar, the only game in town is O Lagar de Jesus. We've written about it in more detail here. But we loved this Albergue and all its trappings.

Day Five: Vilar to Santiago

Vilar is the perfect distance from Santiago. Approx four hours of walking today means if you're up early, you can be in Santiago for lunch time or to attend the Pilgrims mass at the Cathedral.

Distance: 19km

Highlights: Cafes on route filled with Pilgrims and good vibes as everyone excitedly marches into town!

Route: The route is not unpleasant, but you'll notice the approach to Santiago as the scenery becomes more industrial. There's excellent camaraderie on route today (despite rain threatening on the day we walked). Pilgrims are everywhere walking in unison and enjoying coffee and last-minute socialising. It's truly special! A couple of hills take you into Santiago. A couple of kms of trails but mostly road.

Food and Accommodation: Santiago has many places to stay and you're spoilt for choice for food. We like The Last Stamp Hostel as its modern and spacious. Look carefully for Menu del Dia options (they do exist in Santiago) or if you are after something fancy, then head to one of the wonderful restaurants on Rua de Ameas like Abastos 2.0.

You can read more about Santiago in a later chapter.

The last 100km of the Camino Frances – from Sarria to Santiago

The path from Sarria to Santiago is the last 100km of the Camino Frances (The French Route of the Camino de Santiago.) The last 100km of the Camino Frances is notable because the Camino Frances is the most popular Camino route. So, if you join this route, you'll be joining the party all the way to Santiago!

How to get to Sarria?

If you're starting your Camino adventure in Sarria,

you might be wondering how to get there.

From Santiago de Compostela, it will take you around 2 hours 30 minutes to get to Sarria. There is no direct bus from Santiago, but you can change in Lugo and take another bus. If you're coming from A Coruna, you can also take a bus to Lugo and change from there. Lugo is around 30 minutes' drive from Sarria, so if you can't get a bus, you could get a taxi.

Where to get a credential in Sarria?

If you are starting your Camino journey in Baamonde and want to get a Compostela in Santiago, then you will need to get a Credential before you start.

There are two options, you can order a credential online through the appropriate pilgrim organisation in your country. Or you could collect your credential in Sarria.

There are a number of places you can collect a credential in Sarria – either one of the many pilgrim albergues, churches or at Monastery of la Magdaelena.

Is the last 100km of the Camino Frances hard?

If you've walked the entire Camino Frances, you will likely find the last 4 or 5 days into Santiago to be quite a breeze! However, if you are walking just the last 100km and you are not a regular multi-day hiker, then you might find some aspects challenging.

There are some ascents and descents on the road from Sarria to Santiago, but nothing significantly steep. The terrain under foot is generally good too. We particularly liked that there were lots of routes through shaded trees, which is very welcome in summer months.

Finally, as the last 100km of the Camino Frances is the most popular route, you will notice that it is quite busy in peak months. This makes for a really congenial and fun atmosphere. It also means that there are extremely regular places to stop for drinks and food in cafes and restaurants. So you should never worry about running out of fuel!

How many days does it take to walk the last 100km of the Camino Frances?

The total distance from Sarria to Santiago de Compostela is 114km. This is most frequently completed by walkers in five days, but there is an option to do it in four if you are comfortable with walking 30km days. Otherwise, you could take six or seven days if that is more appropriate for your pace and goals.

The last 100km of the Camino Frances: From Sarria to Santiago walking stages

As mentioned above, you can choose to walk the last 100km into Santiago over five or four days.

This is most common, but others choose to walk it at a slower pace and enjoy the scenery. We've set out the most common options below. But, as there are so many albergues on route, you could choose to carve up the distance in lots of different ways. There are also no significant or big towns on route, so you can be quite flexible about where you choose to stop.

Five Day Option

Stage One: Sarria to Portomarín 22km
Stage Two: Portomarín to Palas de Rei 25 km
Stage Three: Palas de Rei to Arzúa 29 km
Stage Four: Arzúa to O Pedrouzo 20 km
Stage Five: O Pedrouzo to Santiago de Compostela 20 km

Four Day Option

Stage One: Sarria to Gonzar 30.5km
Stage Two: Gonzar to O Coto 25km
Stage Three: O Coto to Salceda 31.5km
Stage Four: Salceda to Santiago de Compostela 27km

Where to stay on the last 100km of the Camino Frances:

- In Sarria: There are a vast number of albergues to choose from. If you are keen to stay in a municipal one, then check out Xunta de Galicia Sarria (40 beds).

The other popular choice is of course the Monastery La Magdalena, which sleeps 110 people and is a beautiful building. Otherwise, Casa Peltre Hostel is a quaint option with 22 beds.

- In Portomarín: There is a municipal option, Xunta de Galicia Portomarin, it's quite basic but is the largest in the area with 86 beds. You can't book this in advance, so if you want peace of mind then you could book another alternative on Booking.com.
- In Palas de Rei: In Palas de Rei, you have two municipal albergues to choose from – Os Chacotes (112 beds) or Palas de Rei Xunta de Galicia (60 beds). Neither can be booked in advance. There are plenty of private options too!
- In Arzúa: Arzua has a municipal albergue (46 beds) as well as a number of private options that you can book in advance. Do be aware that Arzua is where the North Route joins the French route, so Arzua can get busy.
- In O Pedrouzo: O Pedrouzo is another popular stop, so there are multiple places to stay. A municipal albergue (126 beds!) and a few privates. Look out for Albergue Mirador de Pedrouzo if you're keen for a swimming pool! (You can book on booking.com)

- Where to stay on the last 100km of the Camino Frances (4 day option):
- In Gonzar: There are three options in Gonzar – the municipal albergue (28 beds), Gonzar or Casa Garcia Hostel.
- In O Coto: O Coto is not the most popular stop on the last 100km of the Camino Frances (because most people follow the five day walk and don't stop here.) But there is one good albergue and a pension, however there are no municipal options here so it is a little more expensive.
- In Salceda: Salceda has another great option with a swimming pool, Albergue Turistico Salceda (on booking.com too), otherwise there are a couple of small pensions and albergues.

The last 100km of the Camino del Norte - From Baamonde to Santiago

Baamonde to Santiago is the last 100km of the Camino del Norte. The Camino del Norte merges with the Camino Frances route within the last 100km to Santiago. So you'll get to walk a bit of the French route too!

How to get to Baamonde?

If you're starting your Camino adventure in Baamonde, you might be wondering how to get there.

From A Coruna Bus Station, you can take a direct bus with Alsa buses to Baamonde. This takes approximately 1 hour and 20 minutes. Alternatively, from Santiago you can take a bus to Baamonde that takes around 2 hours.

Where to get a credential in Baamonde?

If you are starting your Camino journey in Baamonde and want to get a Compostela in Santiago, then you will need to get a Credential before you start.

There are two options, you can order a credential online through the appropriate pilgrim organisation in your country. Or you could collect your credential at the pilgrims albergue in Baamonde.

Is the last 100km of the Camino del Norte hard?

If you've walked from Irun to Baamonde, you are not likely to find the last 100km particularly hard. But if this is your first time walking a long distance on a multi-day hike, you may find this challenging. However, the route into Santiago is not particularly challenging terrain. If you take 5 days to walk to Santiago and you've done some training, you will hopefully be able to enjoy the route and it won't feel too strenuous.

There is a choice of routes at Toar, the original route or the new route. The original route is

8km longer than the other. If you want to get your Compostela, it's important that you take the longer route (if you're walking just from Baamonde) as otherwise, you will walk less than 100km into Santiago.

Both routes are comparable in difficulty (apart from the distance) and both are beautiful routes. If you want to try to find the elusive wax stamp for your credential, then you will need to take the longer route.

How many days does it take to walk the last 100km of the Camino del Norte?

The exact distance from Baamonde to Santiago is 102km. On average, most people walk this distance in 4 or 5 days, but you can take longer should you wish to.

There are lots of different ways to walk the last 100km. We've highlighted three possible options below.

The Camino del Norte route joins the Camino Frances at Arzua. The terrain doesn't change much at this point, but you'll notice that the path does get busier. This also means that there are more frequent cafes and restaurants along the route.

Some of the last day into Santiago is on road walking, which is not the most fun. But, it's difficult to be dragged down by the terrain because the atmosphere into Santiago is so electric!

The last 100km of the Camino del Norte: From Baamonde to Santiago walking stages

Between Baamonde and Santiago, you will have a choice of two routes, as well as a choice over how many days you take to walk the route you choose. There is a junction at Toar (just after Baamonde) where you have the option to take the original Camino route to Santa Leocadia (Miraz) or the newer route to A Pobra de Parga (As Cruces). The original route is 40km, whilst the shorter route is 32km.

Option One Five Days

Stage One: Baamonde to Miraz 15.5 km
Stage Two: Miraz to Sobrado dos Monxes* 24.5 km
Stage Three: Sobrado dos Monxes to Arzua 22 km
Stage Four: Arzua to O Pedrouzo 20 km
Stage Five: O Pedrouzo to Santiago de Compostela 20 km

Option Two Four Days

Stage One: Baamonde to Miraz 15.5km
Stage Two: Miraz to Sabrado dos Monxes 22km
Stage Three: Sobrado dos Monxes to A Salceda 33.5km
Stage Four: A Salceda to Santiago 28km

Option Three Alternative Four Days

As an alternative four-day route, we chose not

to stay in Baamonde and instead walked from Albergue O Xistral (before Baamonde) to Parga taking the new Camino route from Toar. This was over 40km in one day to walk, so it was strenuous. But, we were able to stay at two of our favourite Albergues on the route. This can be an option if you want to avoid staying overnight in Baamonde.

*In Sobrado dos Monxes, there are two highlights. Firstly, the monastery (Sobrado dos Monxes Pilgrim Hostel), which is a stunning place to stay. Secondly, there is an outdoor swimming pool in the town that costs a couple of euros to enjoy. On a sunny day after a long hike, this is a dream!

Where to stay on the last 100km of the Camino del Norte?

- Baamonde Xunta de Galicia Pilgrims Hostel: A basic albergue with 94 beds and costs 8 euros
- San Martin Pilgrims Hostel (Miraz): A small albergue with 26 beds
- Sobrado dos Monxes Pilgrims Hostel: A monastery albergue with 98 beds and costs 8 euros
- Lecer Hostel is an alternative in Sobrado dos Monxes: an alternative family run albergue if you choose not to stay at the monastery
- Xunta de Galicia Arzua Pilgrims Hostel: A popular albergue with 46 beds that cots 8

euros
- Arca do Pino Xunta de Galicia Pilgrims Hostel (Pedrouzo): A large and popular albergue with 126 beds
- Albergue Turistico Salceda (Salceda): this private albergue has a swimming pool and is a fun place to stay on your last night.

What is the Camino Finisterre?

The Camino Finisterre is the only Camino route in Spain that does not end in Santiago. It has its own route map, way markers and Albergues. But most people walk to Finisterre after completing another route to Santiago.

Finisterre is often referred to as "the edge of the world" (the Latin etymology is Finis Terrea meaning end of the world.) Legend has it that the Romans really did think it was the end of the earth. It is also described as the most Westerly point of Spain. Finisterre is also quite a big deal in Maritime history and in popular culture (having featured in three movies.)

You'll hear Finisterre also referred to as Finisterre (The Galician translation.) The Cape of Finisterre (literal edge) is around 3km from Finisterre town, which is important to note when booking Albergues and making your walking plans.

How long is the Camino Finisterre?

The Camino Finisterre is the shortest Camino at 90km. It can be walked in 3 days at an average of 30 km per day, or over a long period if you want to walk less than 30km per day.

Who walks the Camino Finisterre?
Walking to Finisterre has some interesting connotations. I'd heard various stories. Including "its only the hardcore hippies who walk there,""everyone goes there to burn their bras/passports/shoes"etc. I also expected that it would be quiet, just a few solitary pilgrims walking on past Santiago and refusing to believe that their Camino was over.

Let me tell you, it is not that! Its mainstream and popular and busier than the Norte and Portuguese route combined. I walked it in October, in the pouring rain. But even as I battled against the elements and carried on West, there were other Pilgrims as far as the eye can see. I did spot a few hardcore hippy types, they all looked equally baffled and imagine were thinking "Dude, this has changed"as they saw coach loads of tourists arrive to the Cape.

Why walk the Camino Finisterre?

1. It extends your Camino experience

2. It's fun and Finisterre itself is a good place to party and celebrate your achievement

3. There are some incredible walking trails and scenic views - better than many days we walked on the Camino Portuguese

4. You will metaphorically reach the end! For many people, arriving in Finisterre feels more emotional than the arrival into Santiago.

Itinerary for walking the Camino Finisterre

As the Camino Finisterre is 90km long, you could walk it in three of four days comfortably. Or longer if you prefer. We had three days available so chose to walk roughly 30km each day, which worked really well around Albergues and also lunch stops. We also chose to stay an extra day in Finisterre so that we could recoup and walk to Faro Finisterre to enjoy the sunset properly.

Day One: Santiago to A Pena 29km

Highlights: Crossing the bridge in Ponte Maciera. Woody trails on the run up to A Pena are stunning.

Route: It is quite an up and down day with a large hill just on the run up to A Pena. There are around 13km on trails today, which we loved. Some small towns on route to replenish for food and drinks before going on the way.

Food and accommodation: We stayed in a private room in A Pena at Albergue Alto Da Pena. It is a cafe/albergue serving yummy food and drinks and a nice clean and restful place to stay just a few steps up from the Camino trail.

Day Two: A Pena to Logoso 28km

Highlights: Stunning day of trails. Highlight was definitely the couple of kms into Logoso with views of the river, even in the rain.

Route: A few small hills but mostly you are already at high elevation for the entire route. 7kms of trails and the rest "road" but many are quiet. Theres a cafe around 6km into the morning for breakfast if you've skipped it at the Albergue. Then a few small cafes along the way.

Food and accommodation: We stayed at Albergue O Logoso and it was great. Bunk beds with curtains for around 13 Euros and enjoyed a 3 course dinner with wine for 14 Euros. Home cooked and delicious.

Day Three: Logoso to Finisterre 30km

Highlights: Stunning 13km long trail through the forest. You feel like you're isolated and on top of the world, even when the trail is busy. Look out for the Vakner statue. Legend has it that early Pilgrims in-between 1450 – 1490 found the Vakner creatures (pre dating Weerwolves) guarding the route to Finisterre.

Route: 13 to 14km after Logoso is on a trail. This is absolutely stunning but there is nowhere to get food and water. After that, you drop into the coastal path and the route is mostly flat into Finisterre. Plenty of nice cafes and bars on route for lunch.

Food and Accommodation: Finisterre has a Municipal Albergue that is central to town. We stayed at Albergue La Paz, which is cheap and comfortable. For food, we liked the Menu Del Dia at Rombos restaurant. There are a few late-night bars for partying.

The end of the land, or the tip of Finisterre is actually 3km from the centre of town. The Albergues and most hotels are in the town (although one solitary hotel is built at the end of Cape.)

The walk up has a sturdy path, with incredible views of the coast as you meander up. There's a lovely bar at the top and a few souvenir shops (yes, seriously!)

Our tip – pack a picnic and head up to watch sunset! Don't be in a rush, take your time up there and enjoy!

How to get from Finisterre to Santiago

You could walk of course! The arrows mostly point you all the way back to Santiago.

Alternatively, book a bus through Monbus.es. They run around 4 to 5 times per day, take 3 hours and cost around 7 Euros.

CHAPTER FOURTEEN: WHAT TO DO IN SANTIAGO DE COMPOSTELA

When you arrive in Santiago, you will want to take some time at the Cathedral to celebrate the end of the walk and take a moment to reflect. But what else should you do in Santiago and how much time should you spend there?

Go to the modern art museum

The contemporary art centre of Galicia is a small modern art exhibition centre closer to the middle of Santiago. This gallery is free to enter and will take you an hour or so to walk around. It's worth visiting for the beautiful building, as well as to see the art. There's also a coffee shop on site which is a nice place for a cup and a break.

Visit the Cathedral

The Cathedral in Santiago is absolutely the centrepiece of the city. No visit to Santiago is complete without seeing the cathedral. You can attend a mass, which happens multiple times per day. Be aware that there are often long queues to get into mass. Alternatively, just enjoy the surroundings of the cathedral or visit when a service is not taking place.

Without a doubt, one of the best things to do in Santiago is to sit in the square outside the cathedral and watch the other pilgrims complete their Camino. This is such an emotional experience, and you can feel the joy from everyone arriving to the Cathedral in Santiago.

Learn more about the Pilgrimage

The Museum of Pilgrimage is a great educational experience if you want to learn more about the Camino de Santiago. Anyone who has walked the Camino is given free entry to this museum. Otherwise, there is a small fee. Spend a few hours here exploring the exhibits that are set across three floors.

See the Galician cultural centre

The Galician cultural centre is a nice surprise in Santiago. Although there is not much to see at the centre, the attraction of it is the fascinating design of the buildings. It is a little walk out of town and up a hill, but you are rewarded with excellent views back to the city.

Visit the Santiago University Library

The Santiago University Library is an exquisite building in the heart of the city. Visit to pop in and see the quad for a few minutes. Inside, the library is not hugely exciting as it's used by students daily, but it is worth a visit.

Best wine bars in Santiago de Compostela

Wine is to Santiago as beer is to Munich, this city is full of fantastic bars to enjoy a glass of wine.

Here are our top four favourites near to the Cathedral:

1. Bar Vino (Praza de Mazarelos) Spain is a wine bar with one of the most extensive choices of wine by the glass in Santiago. We loved this place for the variety and the cheese boards too.

2. Botafumerio (Rúa da Acibecheria) one of our favourites because its super buzzy and the staff are very friendly. Prices are reasonable and the tapas free flowing. Expect to go here for one and stay for a few more.

3. For live music, we like A Gramola (Praza de Cervantes). The wine list is not extensive, but this is a small, dark wine bar where you can get stuck in for the whole evening. Just note, it is cash only.

4. Benboa Compostela (Rúa do Preguntoiro) a restaurant serving wine. Come here for a nice glass of Rioja seared alongside excellent smoky chorizo tapas. We loved the low lighting and romantic vibe here.

Best coffee shops in Santiago de Compostela

There is no shortage of coffee shops in Santiago, here are our favourite four:

1. Le Flor (Rúa das Casas Reais) is a cafe serving food and excellent coffee. Best for low key vibes and some interesting decor.

2. Ratinos Coffee Shop (Praza de Entrepraciñas) is possibly the best spot in Santiago for any coffee snobs. Here you can choose from a variety of specialist coffees in a hipster cafe.

3. Pepa A Loba (Rúa do Castro) is a bar restaurant serving excellent cafe con leche in a fun setting near to the Cathedral. This place serves huge plates of brunch and is popular with locals and tourists alike.

4. Cafe Venecia (Rúa do Hórreo) is an

old school Spanish coffee house, serving locals a brisk cup of coffee. Come here to see well-heeled Santiago residents enjoying a drink.

Best restaurants in Santiago de Compostela

1. For fancy tapas: Abastos 2.0 (Praza de Abastos) a fancy tapas place selling interesting twists on Galician tapas in a market stall setting.

2. For Michelin Star: Casa Marcelo (Rúa das Hortas) is one of the Michelin star restaurants in Santiago. It comes highly recommended for the fusion Japanese and Spanish food and bright decor.

3. For low key lunch: Mama Peixe Taberna (Rúa da Algalia de Arriba) near to the Cathedral offers an inexpensive and very popular lunch time set menu. This place specialises in seafood and is a local favourite. Be sure to book a table!

How long do I need in Santiago de Compostela?

Santiago de Compostela is a beautiful city. The small size of it comparative to other Spanish cities means that it is perfect for a weekend break. That said, every time we have been, we have found more things to do and always wanted to stay longer. 48 hours is the minimum time you should spend in Santiago de Compostela to enjoy the main attractions ideally.

Where to stay in Santiago de Compostela

For a budget traveller: The Last Stamp Albergue (Rúa do Preguntoiro) is our favourite hostel to stay in within Santiago. It would be difficult to get closer to the Cathedral than this hostel is. Besides, the beds are spacious and shower facilities are good. Prices are around $25 per person for a bed.

For a budget hotel: We like Pension Santa Cristina (Rúa da Porta da Pena). This small, clean and friendly hotel is extremely close to the cathedral and offers rooms for around $50 per night for two people.

A mid-range hotel: Denike Grupo Atalaia (Rúa da Porta da Pena) is a central hotel with a design feel. The rates start at around $100 per night. Guests here love the location, the staff and the comfortable and quiet rooms.

A luxury option: The Parador in Santiago (Praza do Obradoiro) is an excellent luxury option. This hotel will set you back around $250 per night but is right next to the Cathedral in a 15th century stunning building. Part of the well-known Parador chain, this particular hotel offers one of the most central locations compared to others.

SECTION THREE: AFTER THE CAMINO

"All truly great thoughts are conceived by walking." – Friedrich Nietzsche

CHAPTER FIFTEEN: WHAT NEXT?

The Immediate Aftermath

As soon as you arrive in Santiago, a few things might happen. Arriving at the Cathedral could be incredibly emotional for you, or it could leave you feeling a sense of emptiness, or even with no reaction at all. Many people choose to walk on to Finisterre and find more of an emotional feeling once they arrive there. Personally, I'd recommend doing this if you can – it's a truly beautiful route and well worth the extra couple of days if you have it (see previous chapter for more information). Alternatively, you might want to take a few days to soak up Santiago and party hard (see previous chapter for a guide to Santiago).

Many people report feeling a "Post-Camino Dip". Suddenly, you wake up the day after the Camino and you have nowhere to walk. That can be really unsettling and can take time to adjust. Of course, many people immediately have to return to work or normal life and are left feeling as though the experience they had on the Camino is a million miles away.

All feelings are normal!

Based on research and my own experience, here are a few things that might happen in the medium term after completing the Camino.

Finding Answers

A lot of people walk the Camino looking for answers to specific questions. For example, what to do at a particular point in their careers. Often, they may not find the answer to these questions, but other questions come up and the answers unfold. I've heard that often times, the thinking time afforded to Pilgrims, can act as almost like a personal therapy. Sometimes, by the end of the walk, one has spent so much time analysing, that it's not uncommon to start to identify patterns in your behaviour. Similar to how you might identify behaviours through sessions with a talking therapist or psychoanalyst. However, many people also find that it takes time for the lessons they've learned during the Camino to percolate. This is where a journaling practise during the Camino can help you. But if you haven't done that, it can be helpful to take some time after the Camino to reflect on your experience and the emotions and thoughts that came up for you along the way.

Finding Confidence

Setting out to complete a massive physical, emotional and mental challenge and completing it, can create immense feelings of confidence. Perhaps you complete the Camino and lose weight that you have been trying to lose for a long time, or perhaps you feel fitter and stronger than ever. The changes to your body that you will undergo can give you a new sense of confidence. Or, maybe you're a shy person and had to push yourself out of your comfort zone to socialise and share space with lots of new people during the Camino. Achieving your goals in this space might also give you a new lease of life. Even just completing the Camino, knowing that you set your mind to it and DID IT! That will give you new confidence if you let it.

Finding New Community

You will meet people from all different backgrounds on the Camino. You might start a new romantic relationship, or make some new life long friends. Many people report finding new community and this changing their social interactions for good. Even if you don't make lots of close friends, just being part of the Camino community can be enough to help nudge you to meet different people once you return home. Perhaps joining a hiking club, or meeting like minded people. A number of people also choose to volunteer in some capacity on the Camino, continue to engage with it in some way, or indeed write a book about it!

Finding New Direction

With new found confidence and perhaps some answers to some of your questions, a new direction might beckon after the Camino. There are lots of stories about people making big career changes, moving to different countries and starting or ending relationships after walking the Camino. Other people might make small changes, perhaps taking on a new hobby or making a long term commitment to health and fitness. Whatever it is, if you continue to follow your nose and take one step at a time (just like on the Camino) you can continue in a brand new direction after the Camino.

What to do next?

Here are some ideas as to what you could do next to keep up the Camino high and continue on your way.

One: Another Camino

Ride the momentum and schedule another Camino. After my first one, I had booked flights to start my second one within 18 days. The Camino will always be here for you, but there's no time like the present. You could also try to bring a friend from home or introduce someone new to the Camino. If you've done a Camino in Summer, why not try walking in a different season? Or, try a new route.

Two: Engage with the Camino Community

You could start following Camino blogs or social media accounts, or start your own blog. There is so much content out there to engage with if you'd like to. Alternatively, you can volunteer with a Friends of the Camino association, or get in touch with your favourite Albergue and ask if you can help out in any way.

Three: Alternatives to the Camino

Of course, the Camino is truly special. But, if you really feel you've been bitten by the long-distance hiking bug when you finish the Camino, then the following long-distance hikes in Europe are worth checking out.

Short Multi-Day hikes in Europe

West Highland Way (Scotland)

About this trail: The West Highland Way, referred to as "Scotland's best-loved hike"is a 96-mile trail. Starting near to the city of Glasgow and ending in Fort William, it passes varied terrain, including Loch Lomond. This is a really established trail, walked by many each year. It's so well organised that you can even buy a West Highland Way passport.

Accommodation: There are hostels (bunk houses), B&Bs and hotels on route. And of course, the famous Scotties Bothies! The other popular option is to wild camp, which is legal in Scotland.

Distance/ duration: The West Highland Way is 96 miles/ 154km which will take 5 to 7 days to walk depending on your pace. If you don't have time to do the full distance, there are shorter routes available too.

Best time of year: The best times of year to walk the West Highland Way are May, June, September and October

The Camino Ingles (England)

About this trail: OK, we haven't fully moved away from the Camino. But, I bet you've never heard of this! There is a section of the Camino de Santiago in England. This trail has very recently been sign posted and is open for business. It's the start of the Camino Ingles trail, which continues from A Coruna in Northern Spain, eventually joining Santiago.

In the South of England, you will start this trail in Reading before travelling across English countryside and visiting the city of Winchester, famous for it's Cathedral. Eventually, you will end up in Southampton, a port city.

Fun fact – if you complete this trail (and get your pilgrim passport stamped) you can continue to the Camino Ingles in Spain (after a ferry ride) and walk to Santiago to get your Compostela. This is the only way to walk the Camino Ingles and qualify for your certificate.

Accommodation: There are no "official" pilgrim accommodation options, but plenty of good old fashioned English bed and breakfasts along the way. Did I mention there are 13 pubs on the trail too?

Distance/ Duration: The Camino from Reading is 68 miles/ 105 km which will take 3 to 5 days depending on your pace

Best time of year: The best time of year to walk the Camino Ingles English section is April to October

Long distance hikes in Europe that take around 14 days

The GR20 (Corsica)

About this trail: Widely thought to be one of the most challenging trails in Europe, the GR20 runs through the lower mountains of Corsica. It can be tricky to navigate and even trickier to walk, but it's hugely popular with hikers. It's not difficult to understand why it is so popular, Corsica is a beautiful island and the GR20 provides a challenging adventure for adrenaline chasers.

Accommodation: The accommodation on the GR20 is a mix of basic mountain refuge huts and bergeries (dorm style accommodation). There are also hotels at the start and the end of the route. Finally, you can choose to camp – either packing and carrying your own tent, or renting them daily from the mountain huts.

Distance/ Duration: The GR20 is 112 miles/ 180km. The entire GR20 will take two weeks to walk. But, you can walk the GR20 South or GR20 North, which is half the trail and takes half the time.

Best time of year: The best time of year to walk the GR20 is May to October. During the winter, the trail is likely to be covered in snow.

Via Francigena (Italy)

About this trail: This route takes you from the charming town of Lucca, through Siena and the golden Tuscan countryside all the way to Rome. It's a 400km section of the 2000km Via Francigena, which starts in Canterbury and ends in Rome.

Many people talk about the Via Francigena as an alternative to the Camino de Santiago, but it is quite different. Although the premise is similar– it's a pilgrimage to a holy site–the scenery and Italian culture are a marked contrast to the Camino.

We've heard that this is the prettiest stretch of the Via Francigena, plus, what can be bad about walking through vineyards in Tuscany?

Accommodation: There is pilgrim accommodation available as well as tourist hotels and B&Bs along the route from Lucca to Rome on the Via Francigena.

Distance/ Duration: The distance from Lucca to Rome on the Via Francigena is 260 miles/419 km. This will require around 14 to 18 days of walking depending on your pace.

Best time of year: The best time of year to walk the Tuscany leg of the Via Francigena (Lucca to Rome) is March to October, but you may wish to avoid peak summer.

The Trans Caucasian Trail (Armenia, Georgia and Azerbaijan)

About this trail: The Trans Caucasian Trail really excites us, because it travels through a few countries that we haven't yet had the pleasure of visiting. The TCT is a path (in the making) through Georgia, Armenia and Azerbaijan. At time of writing, you cannot yet thru-hike the entire trail. But, sections are opening regularly, with volunteers working passionately to unveil new paths for future hikers.

At present, the TCT officials are allowing a small number of hikers to thru-hike the 800km across Armenia, but currently this is described as a challenging route only available for self-sufficient hikers comfortable with the risk of walking a new trail with minimal infrastructure.

There are however some sections already open. There's a 10 day stretch open in Georgia, a 10 day stretch in Azerbaijan and a 12 day trail open in Armenian.

Accommodation: Along the sections of the Trans Caucasian Trail that are open, there is a mix of some guest house accommodation or camping. If opting to hike across Armenia, you will only be able to camp on the route.

Distance/ Duration: As noted above, the full Trans Caucasian Trail is not yet open, but you can walk sections of it in 10-12 day durations.

Best time of year: The best time of year to walk the Trans Caucasian Trail is June to October.

E4 Path (Cyprus)

About this trail: The E4 is one of Europe's long distance paths. Starting in Gibraltar, it runs through Spain, France, Germany and a number of other countries before arriving in Cyprus.

The Cyprus section itself is around 500km and

takes hikers from Larnarca airport to Paphos airport. Picture coastal walks followed by a dip in the clear blue water and a glass of local wine in the evening.

Accommodation: Accommodation on the E4 in Cyprus includes agritourism places and B&Bs. Sections of the route route are in touristy areas, therefore there are hotel options on some of it too. You can also camp at various campsites or wild camp along the route.

Distance/ Duration: The total path is around 500km, but you can walk sections of it instead. The coastal path around Paphos and sections of the Aphrodite trail are said to be the most beautiful.

Best time of year: The best time of year to walk the E4 around Cyprus is April to October, but expect high temperatures in peak summer.

The Southwest Coast Path (England)

About this trail: After reading the Salt Path by Raynor Winn, I am enamoured with the idea of walking the Southwest Coast Path. This year marks the 50th anniversary of the path and what could be a better way to celebrate it than stomping along it?

The trail runs through some of the most stunning areas of England including Dorset, Devon and Cornwall. It starts in Minehead and ends in Poole, having wrapped around Lands End in Cornwall on the way.

Picture sweeping coastlines, rugged scenery and a pint of cold cider to end your day.

Accommodation: The Southwest Coast Path has a number of B&Bs and hotels along the way. There are also numerous campsites, where you can pitch a tent for a small price.

Distance/ Duration: The Southwest Coast Path is 630 miles/ 1014 km. Therefore, to walk the entire trail would take over one month. But you could walk half of it, or a section of this path easily in a shorter time period.

Best time of year: The best time of the year to walk the Southwest Coast Path is June, July and August

Coast to Coast (England)

About this trail: The Coast-to-Coast Trail crosses the belly of England, from the West to the East. It winds through the Lake District and the Yorkshire Dales before ending in Robin Hood's Bay.

The walk is thought to have been founded by Alfred Wainwright in the 1970s. He famously remarked of the Coast to Coast "Surely there cannot be a finer itinerary for a long-distance walk!"

Accommodation: There are B&Bs, youth hostels

and hotels along the coast to coast route. However, you are recommended to book these well in advance as the coast to coast is a popular walk that runs through tourist areas.

Distance/ Duration: The entire Coast to Coast path is 190 miles/ 305 km, it can be walked in around 14 days depending on your pace.

Best time of year: The best time of year to walk Coast to Coast in the UK June, July and August.

Rheinsteig (Germany)

About this trail: The Rheinsteig is a trail that skirts alongside the river Rhine through Bonn, Koblenz and Wiesbaden. It is mostly a narrow path with some steep climbs. You'll find a mix of cities, like Bonn, juxtaposed with the vineyards abutting the river Rhine.

Perhaps the most famous wine of this region is Riesling, a drop of which could be your reward at the end of a good day of hiking. The other bonus to walking this trail is that the Rheinsteig officials boast that there is "Absolutely no chance of getting lost", due to the thorough and clear markings along the trail.

Accommodation: There is a vast selection of accommodation on the Rheinsteig, from hostels, to B&Bs and hotels. Officially wild camping is illegal in Germany, but it's unclear if stealth camping may be acceptable if the usual rules are followed.

Distance/ Duration: The Rheinsteig is 190miles/ 320km and will take between 10 and 14 days to complete, depending on your pace.

Best time of year: The best time of year to walk the Rheinsteig in Germany is March to October

Pieterpad (The Netherlands)

About this trail: The Pieterpad was crated by two Dutch ladies in the early 1980s who were inspired to create a long distance path in The Netherlands. It is a way marked path, starting near to Groningen and ending in Sint Pietersberg to the South, near to the cosmopolitan city of Maastricht.

Of course, The Netherlands is not known for mountainous terrain, the trail is fairly flat. But it flows across countryside that you wouldn't otherwise get a chance to see in The Netherlands. And of course, you can stop at some fun Dutch towns and cities on route.

Accommodation: Bed and breakfasts, hotels and camping options are available along the Pieterpad trail.

Distance/ Duration: The entirety of this trail is 500km (310 miles). You'd be hard pushed to walk this in 14 days, but perhaps could do a section of it, or take a little longer to complete it.

Best time of year: The best time of year to walk the Pieterpad in The Netherlands is April to October

Long distance hikes in Europe that take around one month

Kungsleden (Sweden)

About this trail: Kungsleden literally means Kings Trail. The hike in Sweden is between Abisko and Hemavan. The most exciting thing is that in walking this trail, you cross through Lapland mountains and four national parks.

Accommodation: There are 16 mountain huts on the Kungsleden, but some patches where other accommodation must be relied upon.

Distance/ Duration: The distance of Kungsleden is 270 miles/ 440 km. Although this is not a particularly long trail, it is recommended to walk it in four weeks, due to the difficulty. But, if you have a quicker walking pace you may be able to complete it in less time.

Best time of year: The best time of year to walk Kungsleden Mid-June until Mid-September.

St Olav Ways (Norway)

About this trail: St Olav Ways are actually a series of different paths in Norway. We have our eye on the Gudbrandsdalsleden, which runs from Oslo to Trondheim, which is the most popular of the paths.

This trail takes in two large Norwegian cities at the start and end, as well as passing through small communities and towns. The real selling point is the opportunity to stay in farming communities along the way and enjoy the tranquil Scandinavian countryside.

Accommodation: There are small walkers hostels along the Gudbrandsdalsleden route, it's recommended to book these in advance. There is also the option to wild camp, as this is legal in Norway.

Distance/ Duration: The length of the Gudbrandsdalsleden 643km/ 400 miles. The recommended walking time is 32 days.

Best time of year: The best time of year to walk one of the St Olavs way routes in Norway is May to August

High Scardus Trail (Kosovo, Albania, North Macedonia)

About this trail: The High Scardus is a new hiking trail through the Balkans. Not only is it the newest, but it is also the highest trail in the Balkans, with ascents of up to 2000m.

This is a remote but beautiful trail, with the opportunity to see three countries as you hike. Scenery highlights include Lake Ohrid and Mount

Korab. But mostly, the draw to the High Scardus Trail is the Balkans hospitality that comes with Raki and home cooked food.

Accommodation: There are basic home stays along the way on the High Scardus Trail, these should be booked in advance. Wild camping is also an option (with some restrictions.)

Distance/ Duration: The High Scardus trail is 495km/ 307 miles. 20 days is the recommended duration to walk the entire trail.

Best time of year: The best time of year to walk the High Scardus trail is June to September.

Slovenia Mountain Trail (Slovenia)

About this trail: The Slovenia Mountain Trail runs across Slovenia through alpine routes. This mountainous route is said to be well way-marked and takes in some incredible scenery along the way.

You don't necessarily have to walk the whole way, you can pick sections of it, or walk the length of the trail if you wish to. The highest point of the route is just short of 3000m in Triglav. Highlights include the Julian Alps where unbelievable blue lakes contrast with green pastures.

Accommodation: There are mountain huts at various points along the route. Camping is not allowed on the Slovenia Mountain Trail however.

Distance/ Duration: The distance of the Slovenia Mountain Trail is 599km/ 372 miles. The recommended walking time is 30 days, depending on your pace.

Best time of year: The best time of year to walk the Slovenia trail is June to October

Traumpfad (Germany to Italy)

About this trail: Traumpfad (The Dream Way) is a trail from Munich, in Germany, to Venice in Italy. Crossing the Bavarian foothills and eventually through the Dolomites. There's some significant elevation (of course) but it's rumoured to be a suitable trail for most experienced walkers.

We like the idea of it, because walking from Munich to Venice just sounds like a good idea! It seems like it would be mildly crazy but with a whiff of romance. From beer halls in Germany, to mountain tipples in Austria and spritz by the canals of Venezia. Truly, the Dream Way.

Accommodation: Mountain huts are the name of the game when it comes to accommodation on Traumpfad. Expect group dining and basic facilities, but oodles of Alpine charm.

Distance/ Duration: The Traumpfad is 327 miles/ 526 km long. As this is a mountainous walk, it's difficult to specify a duration but most people would complete it within 30 days.

Best time of year: May to September is the best time of year to walk the Traumpfad.

Closing Statement

To finish things off, why not jot down some notes about your experience and make some commitments to yourself about your next steps.

One thing I learnt about myself when walking the Camino

One thing I loved about myself when walking the Camino

One insight I gained from the Camino

One inspiring person I met

One place I want to return to

One promise I am making to myself now

One change I want to make in my life

One health and wellness commitment I am making

One decision I have made

A MESSAGE FROM LOTUS EATERS TRAVEL

Thank you very much for reading The Camino Survival Guide. We hope that you enjoyed this book and that it helped you to survive and thrive while walking the Camino de Santiago.

Lotus Eaters Travel are a team of travel writers and Digital Nomads. If you would like to read more of our travel guides and writing you can find us at www.lotuseaters.travel.

Buen Camino.

[i]References

Wall Text Exhibit, Museo Das Peregrinacions de Santiago De Compostela, Santiago De Compostela, Spain, October 2022

[ii] Oficina del Peregrino, https://

oficinadelperegrino.com/en/, October 2022

[iii]Oficina del Peregrino, https://oficinadelperegrino.com/en/, April 2023

[iv]Oficina del Peregrino, https://oficinadelperegrino.com/en/, October 2022

[v] Oficina del Peregrino, https://oficinadelperegrino.com/en/, October 2022 April 2023

[vi]Oficina del Peregrino, https://oficinadelperegrino.com/en/, October 2022

[vii]Oficina del Peregrino, https://oficinadelperegrino.com/en/, October 2022

[viii] https://www.magichillholidays.com/celebrites-camino-de-santiago/, October 2022

[ix]https://fastestknowntime.com/route/camino-de-santiago-spain, October 2022

[x] Wall Text Exhibit, Museo Das Peregrinacions de Santiago De Compostela, Santiago De Compostela, Spain, October 2022

[xi]Eat Well Guide, https://www.nhs.uk/live-well/eat-well/food-guidelines-and-food-labels/the-eatwell-guide/, October 2022

Printed in Great Britain
by Amazon